CW00508109

THE ENCHANTED VILLAGE

NEWTON HARCOURT

Erewash Canal Company's motorboat and butty, passing through Newton Spinney Lock in August 1943.

Contents

Introduction

This book records and celebrates the survival and flourishing of a remarkably unchanged and independent village. Its population is no greater today than the figure recorded in the Domesday book of 1086. A noted county beauty spot, it is still possible in Newton to experience a Hardyesque peace and remoteness.

Joe Goddard, writer and countryman, has lived in Newton Harcourt all his life. Growing up in the Manor House and one of Newton's close-knit community of children in the 1950s, he shares his research and his many memories in these pages.

Colin Garratt, author and photographer, famous for his pictures of the world's last steam locomotives, discovered Newton Harcourt and its railway in 1949 when he fell in love with both village and railway. Colin has written and illustrated some 50 books mostly based on his world expeditions and in 1974 he fulfilled a childhood dream to live in Newton Harcourt. He now occupies Elms Farm.

Writing from very different perspectives, Colin and Joe will let the chapters speak for themselves.

Authors Colin Garratt and Joe Goddard.

Village & Manor

By Joe Goddard

In the summer of 1980 the farmer who had the grazing of the 20 or so acres around the manor house at Newton Harcourt urgently needed to find a reliable water supply. The existing arrangement had been unusually erratic and it occurred to him that he might be able to make that huddle of fields entirely self-sufficient for water by tapping into the old (pre-mains) supply to the manor. The land slopes down from there to the little Sence Valley, so it would be a simple matter to plug such water into the field trough network. Gravity would do the rest. It looked easy. But his enquiries revealed a problem – and a puzzle: there was no such reliable supply. This was all the more surprising because a small amount of research suggested that the manor settlement has almost certainly occupied the same site since the 12th century and perhaps earlier. Yet its only recorded water source turned out to be a shallow and silty well from the mid-19th century, that had served the buildings until the late 1950s. Somehow more villagers got drawn into the question that had opened a window onto the story of the whole parish. More searching in the excellent County Records Office in Wigston revealed a village history going back beyond Domesday, with some riveting insights into our community as it has prospered, suffered and evolved over a thousand years – some answers and some tantalising clues. So here's our story as it stands at present.

The New Village

If you travel south from Leicester on the ancient drover's way called the Welford Road (now the A5199), after about three miles you will reach the Saxon crossroads in the village of Wigston Magna. Take the road left to the possible Roman settlement of Fleckney. The pioneer local historian W G Hoskins considered this road to be an unaltered late Saxon route.

Two miles out of Wigston the Saxon road to Great Glen branches to the left to run eastward. A quarter of a mile from this junction it forms Newton Harcourt's main street. Thus the noisiest and busiest thing in our village is probably the oldest. From the middle of Main Street a bridle path runs northwards to join the important Saxon boundary road called Mere Lane. Maps and aerial photographs suggest that this bridleway probably once ran almost straight from Mere Lane to the shrine (later church) of St. Wistan at Wistow.

So Newton Harcourt in its beginnings in late Saxon times ('Newton': new settlement) would have been on or near two important road junctions, servicing the needs of merchants, traders, travellers and pilgrims and also supporting an agricultural population and all its interrelated small industries, the blacksmith, the baker and all the rest that existed into the early 20th century.

The country lane leading up the hill to Newton Harcourt from Great Glen. The pioneer local historian W. G. Hoskins considered this road, which in a mile or so becomes Newton Harcourt's main street, to date back to late Saxon times.

However, although the village today actually straddles the waterless ridge of the main street, it began life a quarter of a mile to the south, inside a substantial rectangular earthwork enclosing about twelve acres. Water is easily accessed here – indeed the east side was bounded by a fair sized stream (diverted when the canal was built, and now much reduced) that also fed the recently discovered manorial fishpond, while the south side is just twenty yards north of the Sence brook. Village, manor buildings and church would have nestled here in the centuries from its birth until around the fifteenth century when successive outbreaks of plague had depopulated the whole area. Church and manor buildings live on, probably exactly where they have always been, within the earth enclosure.

A time-traveller to around the period of the Norman Conquest in 1066 would be shocked by a landscape that probably would not be recognisable at all, except possibly for buildings on the sites of the present-day manor house and St Luke's Church. The Parish contained more arable land (land ploughed for crops) than at any time until the 1940s. This cultivated land lay in long strips in one of Newton's two enormous fields. (These strips have left us the 'ridge and furrow' fields that are still all around the village). One of these fields was always 'fallow' or resting. The strips were allocated to different villagers by the elected village Reeve, who shared out the land according to a villager's status and according to a mass of complex local rules established in the tenth century and which varied from area to area. There

Above: The original site of Newton Harcourt Village. Manor buildings and St Luke's Church still within the original village site a quarter of a mile from the present village.

Left page: A reconstructed Saxon village.

was a considerable amount of sharing of resources such as ox teams for ploughing, firewood from the 'waste' or woodland and grazing of animals in the woods and water meadows. There would have been very few hedges, and trees would have been confined to the marshy river margins of the river Sence (a much bigger watercourse than it is today). This was an intensively farmed countryside - every square yard was used, woodland being coppiced for firewood and also commonly shared for grazing pigs. The open - field system remained in place until the revolutionary private Act of Parliament which ordered its enclosure. This was caused by the Earl of Denby who had married the widow of the Sir Henry Halford of the time and applied to Newton, Wistow, and Kilby in 1772. Today just one parish, Laxton in Nottinghamshire, is still farmed on the open - field principle.

In 1240 Newton Harcourt Parish changed from two fields to three: These would have consisted of one big field of winter - sown wheat, one field of spring-sown barley, peas or that great medieval staple crop, the broad bean for which Leicestershire

was famous. The third field would be resting, probably being manured by grazing animals.

But at some stage, perhaps in the sixteenth century, the village's farms began to move up the hill. Perhaps the farmers wanted to be nearer the Wigston – Great Glen road and could afford the much deeper wells needed for water supply. Air photography shows up old 'closes' (small village fields) on the south side of today's village. These may date from this time and might suggest that the post-plague remnant of the village was moving up from the earthworks. There's also a fine, small moated site (a moat was a status symbol) at the west end of the village which may date from this time. Throughout this period the pilgrims' road and the Wigston Glen road were probably busy: Wigston was already well-established and Great Glen may have been a royal centre of the kingdom of Mercia in Saxon times.

A quarter of a mile east of Newton towards Glen, the road bends to the left. This spot has always been called 'Jacobs Corner'. 'Jacob' can be a corruption of 'jagger', a packhorse

Above: A thirteenth century village

Left page: Village life under the Normans

driver. So this may infer that packhorse teams once passed this way and perhaps rested there.

Newton Harcourt was first documented in the Domesday survey of 1086. It was then the largest of Wistow's three daughter settlements (the other two being Fleckney, two and a half miles to the southeast and Kilby, one and a half miles to the southwest. Before the Norman Conquest in 1066, the area had been an estate owned by Aelric, a Saxon. The village, like many villages called Newton, may date from the late 10th or early 11th century. Wistow as noted was the shrine of Prince Wistan (or sometimes Wulstan) of Mercia, murdered there by his uncle Beorthfrith in 849 AD. There are two entries for "Neutone" in the Domesday Book; one for the village as a whole giving the area of its fields, about 1200 acres and including 'Unum Molinum' – a water mill. The other entry refers to 'Unus Miles' – a man at arms who holds

about 240 acres. It would be nice to think that he coincided with the origins of the manor site, but wrong to claim any such likelihood for that distant and shadowy community.

Newton's population in 1086 was not very different from today, about 200, a sizeable village then, under the overlordship of Robert de Veci. It is interesting to note that Robert kept only Newton Harcourt and Kibworth Harcourt in his own hand, subletting the rest of his widespread Leicestershire estates.

A survey made in 1130 showed that the de Veci manors in the Gartree Hundred (our local ancient "hundred" division of the county) were by now held by a certain Ansketil, possibly an early member of the de Harcourts, as the name Ansketil recurs in that family. They would leave their surname on Newton Harcourt and Kibworth Harcourt. One of them may have built a manor house, which is referred to in a document of 1199.

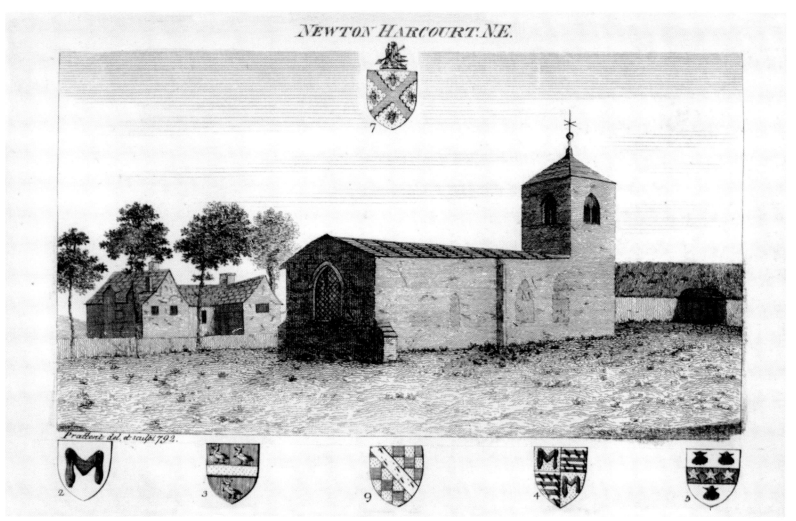

Above: St Luke's Church in 1790. As a chapel - of - ease and not yet a fully consecrated Church it did not have a license for burial, hence no churchyard until 1875.

Left page: Manor buildings and St Luke's Church still within the original village site a quarter of a mile from the present village.

In the 1250s Sir Richard de Harcourt's land including the two Harcourts passed to his son, Saer. Saer de Harcourt had two noticeable shortcomings: financial ineptitude and a serious lack of political judgment. Thus in 1265 we find that Saer's estate has been seized by the Crown as a result of his support for Simon de Montfort's rebellion (mysteriously he'd managed not to be present at de Montfort's final defeat at Evesham in that year). As a result of all this, his forfeited land was being assessed and catalogued by the Crown – giving us a rare glimpse of a small medieval manor. Manor and village were together valued at £20. There was one 'messuage'. referring here, it seems, to a manor house. It had a dovecote, garden, seven and a half virgates (about two hundred and thirty acres) of land and two mills. The mills were together worth 33 shillings and 4 pence. The watermill in the Domesday Book had been joined by a windmill. We can calculate that the watermill was valued at around 23 shillings and the windmill probably at 10 shillings. (A windmill recorded in the 17th century, which stood close to the road to Great Glen, was very probably on the same mound, which was only destroyed in 1975). We can also calculate that the manor house, dovecote and garden were together worth about £8. The lord of the manor directly controlled just under half the parish farmland, the rest being farmed by villeins and free tenants who paid the lord 66 shillings per year and carried out 24 feudal duties, with 46 extra duties to be performed every autumn. The free tenants held seventeen freeholdings and collectively paid £3 annually for these, together with 1lb pepper. (Peppercorns were scarce and valuable and could be used as money. Hence 'peppercorn rent'.)

Newton Harcourt and Kibworth Harcourt must have been closely connected, although their histories diverge from the 1280s onwards. There may have been a road running between the two, a short stretch of which, at Newton, can still be seen at certain times in Highbridge Field. In particular, it seems there were two 'capites', manor houses in the two Harcourts, one being the one on (roughly) the present manor site at Newton Harcourt. We can imagine that the dovecote at Newton contributed pigeon meat (the only reliably obtainable fresh meat in winter) to the ruling family's table while the fish ponds at Kibworth provided the fish which comprised the luxury option for the old Catholic Church rule that meat must not be eaten on Mondays, Wednesdays or Fridays. (Ordinary folk, of course, were supposed to exist on a vegetarian diet). The fishponds still exist, not far from Manor Farm at Kibworth Harcourt, which stands on the probable site of the manor bailiff's house in the days of the de Harcourts. In 1268 Saer de Harcourt was pardoned and his land restored to him. However, there is evidence of shortage of money – he had been heavily fined – and shortly afterwards he began the transfer of his Kibworth Harcourt land to the estate of Bishop Walter de Merton who added it to the assets supporting his newly founded Merton College, Oxford, which has retained much of the farmland to this day. At Saer's death in the late 1270s, his widow, Agnes, claimed the usual one third of his estate as widow's dower (allowance). We read of Agnes later claiming her dower from a new acquirer of the Newton Harcourt land. Saer, as we have seen, had been in financial difficulties at the time of his death and perhaps this newcomer, Walter of Kent, was a creditor. There is no record of where Agnes lived, but it is possible that she lived on in these modest manor houses, if she didn't retreat to the family's main residence at Stanton Harcourt in Oxfordshire, probably the home of her brother in law, Saer's elder brother Richard.

The manor appears to have prospered throughout the latter 13th century and even into the early 14th century with its cold, rainy summers and its famines. However, villeins' and freeholders' rents were reduced in the latter part of the 14th century: a sign that the manor was succumbing to the economic collapse that gripped the country after the Black Death of 1348. The watermill was left out of a survey in 1332 and again in 1436. It seems likely that it disappeared sometime in the 14th century. It is possible that its site has been located in Islands Wood just across the River Sence to the south of the manor house, where there are signs that the old river course silted up and the river then followed the course of the mill stream after the collapse of the mill dam. The survey of 1436, which accompanied a probate inventory upon the death of Richard Hastings, lord of the manor, showed that the whole manor had seriously decayed in the century since the Black Death. The manor's value had reduced to just over £10 and both manor house and dovecote were ruinous. The villeins had apparently ceased performing feudal tasks by then. This may reflect their bargaining power after successive outbreaks of plague had left a labour shortage. Famine and plague led to a steady decline in the village. There were about 63 inhabitants in 1377, but by 1563 there were just twelve households in Newton Harcourt and Fleckney combined.

A New Era of Prosperity

Help came to the manor house in about 1480. The Chamberlain family, prosperous Leicester merchants, began to buy land in the area around Newton Harcourt and Kilby. By the date of William Chamberlain's will of 1535, it is clear that they were very wealthy and living in the manor house where they would remain for 190 years. When a later William Chamberlain died in 1586, his personal estate – including the contents of the house – was valued at £1,376, the equivalent of several million pounds today. It is thought that the Chamberlains' home was simply the tumbled down house described in 1436 much repaired and improved and that this was the forerunner of the house we see today, although two major rebuildings would alter it almost beyond recognition.

Francis Chamberlain purchased the lordship of the manor in 1603 and his son, John, set about rebuilding the manor house in about 1615. Upon his death in 1638 John Chamberlain was the owner of 15,300 bricks (valued at £10) and he was probably planning a more ambitious rebuilding scheme, never realised. What did John Chamberlain's rebuild of 1615 involve? The manor house in 1600 was most likely still a medieval structure (no doubt much patched) of 'cob' (better known in Leicestershire as 'mud'), and some stone structure and stone chimneystacks. This was discovered because cob and old timber and large quantities of stone were excavated when the house was altered below ground level for central heating pipes. One medieval chimney remains and this has recently been fully restored. John Chamberlain replaced the cob with a ground floor of stone from (we think) Tilton, and brick and timber on the first and second floors. He made a thorough job of it and the result was a small manor house in an up-to-date H-plan style, three storeys high. Although it was the centre of a large busy farm, it also had room for a more refined dimension with a walled garden to the east, still there today, and the present main entrance courtyard entered through a stone arch, possibly acquired cheap from a ruined monastery. The fields came up to the south side of the house but on the west side there was probably a formal parterre garden with clipped yew topiary, indicated today by old gnarled yew trees. The medieval kitchen yard seems to have been altered by the addition of a brick wall in place of a crumbling stone wall on its east side and some remains of the de Harcourt house may have been turned into outbuildings, still there. In the course of a visit from the East Midlands Dowsing Association recently, members detected a 45 ft deep stone-lined well just to the west of the kitchen wing established by John Chamberlain. The dowsers considered that it had been filled in, but if excavated it would give 80 gallons per minute. If this is right, it would most likely have been established by the Chamberlain dynasty during the rebuilding. The manor at this point must have been at another apogee as an administrative centre, comparable to its life in the 12th and 13th centuries.

As such it must have witnessed the rout that followed Oliver Cromwell's victory over the Royalist army at the Battle of Naseby twenty miles south in Northamptonshire, in June 1645. Defeated Royalists streamed northwards along every road and lane to their stronghold at Newark Castle, hotly pursued by Cromwellian forces. There was a skirmish along the Wigston - Fleckney road where it is inside the parish, on the stretch known as Watery Lane, and a number of soldiers are believed to be buried in the vicinity.

The Manor in Decline

In 1666 John Chamberlain's widow was assessed for Hearth Tax at ten fireplaces, a fair indication of the family's wealth. The Chamberlains continued at Newton until the end of the 17th century when the estate was acquired by the Halford family of Wistow Hall one mile across the Sence valley. After this the manor house seems to have become a simple farmhouse and all the manor buildings went into gentle decline. In 1789 John Throsby in his History of Leicestershire notes, "There is at Newton Harcourt a large old stone house lived in by a grazier". In 1772, as we have seen, the open-field system was finally ended in Newton Parish by private Act of Parliament. These private Enclosure Acts were affecting almost the whole of England. Nationally, thousands of miles of hedges were planted around new fields based on a ten acre norm, making the landscape we knew until forty or so years ago.

Above: The Manor House was "gentrified" by the Halford family in the 1830s. Before that it had a more forbidding appearance.

*Left page: Mr and Mrs Henry Langton Goddard standing in front of the Manor, with the tennis court in the foreground.
The postcard was posted in Febuary 1902.*

The village meanwhile seems to have recovered from its near extinction in the 16th century. Twenty-two families were once again living in Newton in 1670 and 30 families early in the following century – roughly 180 inhabitants. 186 villagers of all ages are recorded in 1801, 142 in 1931, and in 2004 about 200 – a remarkably stable rise and fall over almost a thousand years. The community never became more than a small village. This has partly been because until recently Newton Harcourt was, as it always had been, a 'closed' estate-controlled village, with little private property expansion. There was also another reason. We find a letter of 1789 addressed to the Wistow Estate from a deputation of disgruntled villagers:

"May it please your lordship, we wose names are here unto set, your lordships tenants and others labor under a perticular disadvantage for want of good water which we are obliged to fetch a considerable way in water carts and then in a wet time muddy and bad. The poor people fetch theirs in yokes and buckets, a great disadvantage."

The Estate's steward replied that he knew of a suitably qualified person able to tap and pipe a spring into the village. Some traces of this system may have very recently been found. Certainly construction in the village began to grow from about this time. About 30 years later the deep village well was sunk in Speck's Lane (now Post Office Lane) and a path led from it to the Square where the village pump was later placed. This supplied the village until 1910 when another private system was established. The villagers continued to rely on these pumps (and to walk about with two buckets suspended from a yoke across their shoulders) until 1953. The Long Row and the Short Row in the central square of the village date from the early 19th century.

Nineteenth century census returns up to 1881 indicate several stocking-frame workers in the village, producing socks for pitifully low wages, on machines ('frames') invented early in the seventeenth century. At 6, Long Row there is still a purpose - built 'knitting shed' where the stocking framer would have worked.

A bizarre tale is attached to No 8 Long Row. This is a ghost story and it is ongoing. For eighty-eight years from 1879 to 1967 the cottage was lived in by Patty Astill, who was born there. Years later, in 1990, the house belonged to author Lucinda Whittaker and her husband Owen, who had just redecorated it. One evening Lucinda was shocked to see a little old lady sitting in the bedroom. The apparition sat there peacefully, then disappeared. This apparently happened several times. In the past few years the present owners , Jackie Toland and Tony Haywood, have had a simular experience, again just after they had altered the cottage. Jackie saw the old lady sitting in the bedroom. She said nothing about it but then she was at a carol singing at the Manor when she noticed a painting by Paticia Goddard, from the 1960s. She said, 'My hair stood on end -- it was a portrait of the same old lady I'd seen sitting in the bedroom.' Jackie asked who the subject of the painting was and found that it was a picture of Patty Astill, who clearly is still taking an interest in No 8.

The Pub in Newton Harcourt

The large building now called Sycamore House which occupies the south side of the Square was once the village pub called 'The Bull' until the Napoleonic Wars when it became a local recruiting centre and its name was changed to 'The Recruiting Sergeant'. The Victoria County History (1960) notes that the design suggests a 17th century origin. It has a semi basement, so may have been built as a pub.

The pub had a colourful history. In 1795 the Leicestershire and Northamptonshire Canal was being excavated to the south of the village. The finance for this enterprise seems to have been sketchy to say the least. Wages were often late, and on one occasion this resulted in a spectacular riot by the entire workforce. After the worst of it, the ringleaders were found in mellower mood in 'The Bull'. As 'The Recruiting Sergeant' it later gained a reputation as a gathering place for lawless folk, notably

Patty Astill in her sitting room at 8 Long Row. Painted by Patricia Goddard in 1965.

the notorious Arnesby poaching gang. Following the death of Thomas Monk, a gamekeeper, in a shootout with the poachers on the canal's Turnover Bridge, towards Kilby Bridge, the pub's license was withdrawn in about 1880 by Sir Henry Halford, the landowner at the time. It survived as an off licence until 1976.

In 1854-55 the Midland Counties Railway arrived in Newton Harcourt. The commotion as the army of Railway diggers descended on the village must have been as great as that caused by the canal navigators sixty years earlier. In particular they had to dig the railway cutting through the village to lessen the long climb from Kilby Bridge to Kibworth facing trains coming south from Leicester. Hundreds of tons of soil were dug entirely by hand - hungry and thirsty work. To supply the diggers' needs Mrs Brunskill, the landlady of 'The Recruiting Sergeant' supplied prodigious quantities of beer. This involved brewing more and faster than she ever had before. The pub brewhouse - now the garage of the house next door - must have steamed and reeked with the gallons of beer bubbling away during the six months the diggers' were in the vicinity. Local farmer Edgar Smart, Mrs Brunskill's grandson, remembered a family story that the beer was still brewing and fizzing as it was delivered in pails to the toiling diggers'. The effects of this laxative refreshment in the toiletless confines of the cutting may be imagined.

The manor buildings seemed to have continued into the early 19th century in a rundown state. A sketch of 1827 shows the back of the house looking very dilapidated. Buildings seem to have fallen down, in particular a large structure, possibly a barn, today a flat space in Manor Spinney. Shortly after this, the Halford family rebuilt the house as a dower house – subsidiary family home – to Wistow Hall. Thus White's Trade Directory, 1846, describes the manor as "a small, neat mansion" and this would suggest that the large decaying house of Throsby's description, 50 years earlier, had been greatly modernised and probably reduced in size. Wherever trenches are dug around the kitchen area large loose lumps of dressed stone are found which may have been dumped at this date. This gentrification of the manor created landscaping, a terraced lawn and a ha-ha to the south of the house

and, interestingly, revived the Chamberlains' old parterre by creating a pattern of granite edged paths and rockeries in that area. The house was in turn used by members of the Halford family or tenanted by farmers. The last farmers, the Turners, created a cobble-bedded sheep wash in about 1850. Unfortunately, it seems that at about the same time they were responsible for building a soakaway 'privy' which appears to have contaminated the old well detected by the visiting dowsers. It was filled in and hurriedly replaced by the well referred to at the beginning of this chapter, which was used until 1958. Thus, it seems began 150 years' water shortage for the twenty acres of 'Manor fields'. Barely adequate for the house and stables, the new well could not supply the fields, too. At this point the farmer broke a bank of the sheep wash, to try and make a cattle drinking-pond. This was only reliable in a wet year as the water now escaped through the access point. The sheep wash was restored in 1983 and is now Manor Pond. The fields were still awaiting their water supply, relying into the 21st century on an ad hoc system of pipes and hoses.

After the departure of the Turners in about 1860, the manor's agricultural role seems to have come to an end. It was lived in by a succession of tenants until Joseph Goddard, a Leicester architect, rented it in 1897. His son and daughter-in-law, Harry and Gertrude, bought the manor buildings and surroundings early in the 20th century. The Goddard family have continued at the manor house. Joseph Goddard was a man of inventive turn of mind and some of his ideas have affected the house and surroundings: He pioneered air heating, which caused several roof fires, and he used filtered canal water for his newly installed radiator central heating and for the new–fangled hot tap water for the one bath. As the canal was not up to providing more water for flush toilets, the toilet in his billiard room was a sand closet of his own design. Pressure on the standard-looking lavatory chain released a measured amount of sand from a chute in the ceiling aimed to plummet precisely down the toilet pan. It was important not to pull the chain whilst seated. Accidents to visitors were not unusual. The manor began to be restored in the 1960s and this continues as will be seen in the next chapter.

The Manor House as a Farmhouse in 1827, as rebuilt by the Chamberlains. In 1791 John Nichols wrote '...
There is a large stone house occupied by a Grazier.'

This picture, taken during the late 1890s, shows Joseph Goddard sitting at the front of the wagonette with Miss Blanche Linwood. Mrs Annie Goddard is sitting behind with two of their grandchildren. The coachman's name was John Hayward.

Same place, same family, different horsepower. Anthony and Annette Goddard with daughter Alice and niece Emily, 115 years later.
Joe Goddard standing where Hayward the coachman was standing in the older picture.

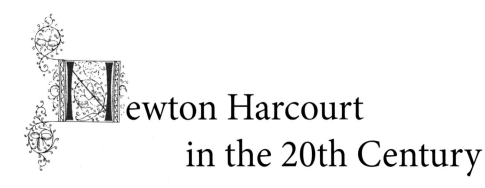

Newton Harcourt in the 20th Century

By Joe Goddard

The village entered the 20th century still firmly an estate-controlled community of feudal character. It largely consisted of five tenant farmers and their farmworkers. There was also a cobbler, three shops including The Post Office, 'Selina Fry's Sweet Shop' in a cob cottage demolished in 1920, the Off Licence (formerly The Recruiting Sergeant) and a smithy (open twice a week) housed in a low building on one side of the square. This interesting structure also contained the village communal bakehouse – and the morgue, of which more in the chapter on St Luke's Church.

When the smithy was not occupied by the blacksmith, two brothers, Horace and Will Dodson, used it as a tiny factory for producing light bicycle oil to a recipe of their own. On Saturday mornings the long brick bakery oven would be filled with dry twigs and small bits of wood and then lit, with the oven door open. As the fire turned to a glow the brick lining could be seen to be shimmering – this showed the bakery was ready for any baking needing a high heat. The embers were raked out and baking would

begin, with a succession of different things to cook as the heat lessened, finishing with some Sunday joints to roast gently over Saturday night.

The main village, Long Row and Short Row and the off licence and the Steward's House, were grouped around the square. Life was simple. All drinking water came from the village pump in the square (still there), though rain water was collected into underground cisterns for washing. Sanitation was also basic: dirty water was saved for the garden, and toilets (called 'privies'), which were situated down the garden, emptied into buckets. Two farmworkers were deputed, for 25p extra wage per week, to empty all the buckets into a horsedrawn cart, then to take the cart to a remote pond and empty it there. They were called "the nine o'clock horseman", and the cart was called "the honeypot"! You can still see "Honeypot Lane" outside many UK villages – this was the lane the cart was driven down for emptying – nothing to do with honey!

Village children dance round the May Pole in the village square on a May day holiday in the 1950s.

The political centre of the village lay down the little alley from the square, called the Jetty. Around this point the farmhouses of Old Croft Farm, Oaks Farm, Old Farm and the Post Office lay just 30 yards from each other. Much business must have been discussed here and the Post Office was the only point of contact with the outside world, through its post and telegram service.

The manor continued much as described in the last chapter. The entire community was lit by daylight, paraffin or candles, and until 1914 all transport was horsedrawn. In April that year the Goddards aquired a car.

The Church of St Luke's was well-attended. The vicar from 1897 to 1946 was Herbert Ransome, a popular figure in Kilby, Wistow and Newton. He had a hatred of wasps and it was considered good fun to waft a stray wasp towards him during a sermon in the summer. An older resident could remember the standing-room-only at Harvest Festivals, the smell of people and paraffin in the warm evening, and two chairs, called "Nipper" and "Pincher", put out for latecomers. They both pinched your bottom when you sat on them!

In 1897 the Wistow Estate had passed from the last Sir Henry Halford to Lord Cottesloe. In 1906 Lord Cottesloe installed a new water supply to a system of about fifteen village pumps. As a result, the village now began slowly to expand as some Wistow Estate houses were built east of the village centre, beside the Glen Road.

Newton Harcourt continued thus until after 1918. Six men from Newton and Wistow died in the Great War, including Private Tom Owens, who died at home in June 1919 as a result of being gassed.

Private electricity came to the Smart family at Old Farm and the Goddards at the Manor in 1919. It was produced by generators powered by paraffin engines and only turned on for a couple of hours on winter evenings and hardly at all in the summer. The Smarts and the Goddards had motor cars – the Ford Model T was the favourite: being high off the ground it was the off-road vehicle of its day. If Jane Austen had visited Newton Harcourt in 1930 she would have seen much of village life unchanged since her

Mr John Wyatt, Gwen Inghams' father, travelling on the road between Newton Harcourt and Wistow. The two magnificent elm trees, once a common feature of the English countryside, have long been lost to Dutch Elm Disease.

Left: This row of cottages was originally built to house farm labourers and their families. They were built by the Halfords of Wistow Hall.

Below: The Square. Short Row (left), Long Row (background) and (right) the village bakery, smithy and mortuary all in one building.

time. A horsedrawn 'carrier' still visited the village with goods and parcels ordered from distant Leicester.

In 1932 electricity came to the village – although not to the Manor until 1938 – and thereafter the pace of life began to change. Charles Martin was a clever eccentric living in one of the new Wistow Estate houses: he built early radios. There were several of these around Newton and the writer believes they were instrumental in bringing about cultural change. After all, you could now hear news from all over Europe and the USA. Edgar Smart of Old Farm bought his first diesel tractor (a single cylinder Marshall) in 1938, but the "9 o'clock horseman" and other horsedrawn jobs would not disappear entirely until about 1958.

So the village arrived at the Second World War, and the fateful year 1940. After the fall of France the war came closer to every doorstep in the land, and Newton was no exception. Although the farming industry remained a 'reserved occupation' (not liable to call-up), a number of villagers had joined the Forces. In December that year villagers gathered at the Wigston Fleckney Road railway bridge and saw the glow and felt the thumps as Coventry was blitzed. A secret drama was also unfolding – a top-secret squad of the Home Guard had been detailed to deliver mortars, machine-guns, rifles and grenades to a point on the Fleckney road between the Wain Bridge (over the little river Sence) and the Canal Bridge (near the scene of the fighting in the Civil War). We now know that in our anti-invasion plans we were to have a Home Guard bunker every 7 miles. All this weaponry was clearly intended for such an H.Q. which if we were invaded, would have been manned by a Home Guard 'suicide squad' – their chances of survival were not good. So where was – or is – this bunker? At a guess, the writer believes, the munitions were collected from the drop-off point and carried down the canal towpath towards Kilby Bridge. There were several characters in the parish who were men of proven bravery from World War One, who might well have been in such a squad, but if so, they have taken the secret with them. After the excitements of that year Newton settled down to the grey routine of rationing, shortages and making do – but as in all country communities, you could circumvent the harsher food privations if you knew a friendly farmer or two.

In both world wars the village had an ingenious way of getting free extra coal. At the point where the railway line south converges with the canal, there is a small field called Ram Close. Villagers used to place rabbit-skins stuffed with straw (to look roughly like rabbits) among the tussocks of Ram Close and the field was always littered with lumps of coal because no fireman on a slow-moving goods train could ever resist throwing a lump of coal at a lineside rabbit!

On the hedge-line near the bridleway up the hill to the north of the village lies the location of part of one of the "Starfish" decoy sites in the Midlands (see map). The Starfish scheme was put in place in 1941 to mislead German bomber crews as to the whereabouts of their target. The decoy consisted of a mountain of combustible material (with more ready for feeding on). If a city or cities in the region had been attacked, the decoy would have been lit and bomber crews might have believed it was the real target. Newton's Starfish was constructed to resemble the railway junction at Knighton. It was never needed, but this scheme had some success elsewhere in Britain.

Newton emerged into the 1950's with its social community largely intact, although the smithy/bakery/morgue was now derelict.

In 1953 a water main was laid (using prison - labour) to the village, and the pumps finally were abandoned. In 1959 Newton received a main sewer and this, with the rapid spread of television, brought the village firmly into the mid-20th century. A much higher standard of living – but an indefinable serenity lost forever. The manor finally received mains water in 1958.

The village began to expand again, slowly, in the mid sixties. This was controlled and localised growth which has made uncontrolled development harder to initiate. At the same time, from the 1980's onwards, there has been a growing awareness of Newton's special situation as a small village in its fields in the midst of an increasingly urban region.

The Long Row in about 1960. The row was built to house farmworkers in the early nineteenth century. The lady walking away from the camera is Gertie Wyatt, Gwen Inghams mother, who lived at No. 2 Long Row. Elms Farmhouse is visible rear left.

20th Century profile: Edgar Smart, Village farmer.
by Joe Goddard

For over 50 years William Edgar Smart was in many ways the symbol of the village and he may be taken as an example of generations of farming families of an outlook and integrity that are passing into history. As the heir to the important and wealthy Smart family of farmers and agricultural contractors, Edgar took over the family business on the death of his father in 1921. Horses provided almost all the farm power, for ploughing, mowing and harvesting – the exception was a Ransomes, Sims and Jeffries traction engine which powered the contract ploughing and threshing machine.

Edgar remained a bachelor all his life although he was rumoured to have had several ladies in tow in his earlier days, and indeed he kept up a close business and social relationship with Georgina Spriggs, farmer, and another strong character. Edgar was a highly intelligent man – for instance, he successfully grew maize decades before this became common. But nobody could have called him tidy; he said that he kept mice in his beautiful farmhouse to tidy up after him, and into the 1970s his lower farmyard was littered with the remains of his forbears' wooden haywains. When he bought a stationary engine in 1930 he paid for it in gold, the Smarts being conservative people. Edgar bought a diesel tractor in 1938. This was a 5.0l single cylinder Marshall 12/20, and thereafter Marshall Tractors replaced horses and the traction engine. As late as 1965 one could hear the steady pop – pop – pop of a Marshall and the hum of a threshing machine all over the village. The Smarts went into home – generated electricity in 1919, the same year as the Goddards at the Manor, but unlike the Goddards the Smarts never threw anything away so that up to Edgar's death in 1976 you could see the 5 horse power Bamford 'Atomic' stationary engine (not atomic at all, running on paraffin), the generator, the stack of glass batteries to take the flicker out of the electric light, and the marvellous lacquered slate switchboard.

Edgar was a notable pig farmer and his pigs were famous for roaming round the (then) empty village lanes. When the houses

Farmer Edgar Smart and Georgina (Georgie) Spriggs. Edgar was a pillar of the community from the end of the First World War to his death in 1976. Georgie Spriggs was another iconic farmer. She and Edgar collaborated in many farming ventures.

Left: A Ward family group, circa late 1920s.

Below: The area Home Guard – officially the Local Defence Volunteers – pose for their official battalion photograph in Highbridge Field, at the back of St Luke's Church. The date is 30 May 1942. Highbridge Plantation can be seen left, behind the group. Dave Collins (fifth from right, front row) recalled that on that night the whole countryside reverberated to the sound of our bombers setting out on "Operation Millenium" – the first thousand bomber raid heading for Cologne.

up to the square were built in the mid-1960s, Edgar's pigs still wandered where they always had, trashing any new fencing that got in their way and then munching the new gardens. Understandably the residents complained to the elderly Edgar who merely said, "I tells them and I tells them, but do they listen…!" Edgar was a last link with the older self-sufficient village.

20th century profile: Walter Tyrrell, Village character. By Joe Goddard

Walter Tyrrell was a typically strong and individual member of the village from the late 19th century to his death in 1963. He was born in Barn Spinney Farm in 1881 and would live in Newton all his life. The census description of 'agricultural labourer' does not do him justice. Village handyman, general gardener, farmworker, smallholder, poacher and village sexton; there can barely have been enough hours in the day for all his activities. In addition he was a famous slow spin bowler in Newton Harcourt's cricket team up to the 1930s and rolled and mowed the cricket pitch long after that.

Perhaps his most interesting job was as the village sexton, a role he filled from about 1900 until 1960. Walter could recite the name of every parishioner for whom he had dug a grave, with particulars of each 'client'. He also had an encyclopaedic knowledge of local dignitaries and people of interest – and by the 1960s some of these people were in the distant past. For instance, Walter could always remember the Firth family who rented Wistow Hall in the late 19th and early 20th centuries. They were iron founders from Sheffield and went about the county in a coach drawn by four horses.

His father John Tyrrell had arrived in Newton from the family's home in Wilbarston, Northamptonshire in the 1870s and Walter had a strange story to tell about his forbears there. Walter firmly believed that his great grandfather had destroyed a witch. The story went that dairy cattle around Wilbarston suddenly became restive and hard to milk. The Tyrrell of those days was appointed to guard the cattle and keep watch at night. One night

Walter Tyrrell despite his short stature, was another giant character. Farmworker and gardener, he was also the parish sexton, and if you had the time he could recite to you the name of everyone he had buried in Newton Churchyard over a period of sixty years. Then he was also the guardian of the church communion plate – which he washed in the canal.

The village school photograpgh for 1928. Gwen Ingam is in the middle row fourth from the right and prophetically at the centre of the group, Bert Sheppards is in the back row, third from right. Both would live in Newton Harcourt all their lives. The teacher was Miss Plumtree.

The Wistow Estate provided the national school building in 1866, for pupils aged from five years to twelve. The school leaving age would rise to fourteen and the school would become a junior school in 1923, finally closing in 1937.

soon afterwards he saw a very large hare jumping around the cows and chasing them. Now in Wilbarston there lived a solitary and unprepossessing old woman (who no doubt kept a black cat). Mr Tyrrell returned to guard the cattle the following night armed with a shotgun. The hare duly appeared and Mr Tyrrell shot and wounded it. The hare limped away and was not seen again. By coincidence no doubt, the solitary old woman was not seen in the village for some days, then finally appeared, limping painfully, before leaving the village for good. Proof positive, Mr Tyrrell always maintained.

There is an odd sequel to this story "The Leicester Chronicle and Leicestershire Mercury", March 13th 1875, carried the following article:

'Newton Harcourt: Freak of Nature'

'A short time since, the wife of Mr John Tyrrell, of this place, gave birth to a fine healthy female child with five fingers and a thumb on each hand. Out of curiosity most of the female inhabitants have been to see it. The child and its mother are both doing well'.

Walter had his own individualistic ways, such as washing St Luke's communion plate in the canal at the bottom of the churchyard – and singing loudly and off key. When a visiting clergyman asked him during a service to turn down the volume he replied loudly, "Bless you, I'm not singing for you, I'm singing for my Maker".

Walter was a last link with the Halford family of Wistow whom he remembered clearly.

20th century profile: Gwen Ingham.
by Colin Garratt

The isolation of Newton Harcourt led to a rich social life within the village during the mid to late years of the twentieth century. Many characters stood out but none more deserving of a place within these pages than Gwen Ingham. It would not be much of an exaggeration to say that the village's social life revolved around her. She kept the village shop and Post Office, she was a leading figure in the Newton Harcourt Women's Institute; she played a prominent role in the church and was a keen organiser of the village's many special events such as Fetes, taking part in the WI, Shrove Tuesday Fancy Dress Dances and numerous street parties. Gwen was so ingrained in the daily life of the community that there was a time in the 1950s when she could walk unannounced into any house in the village; not only were the doors unlocked but she would always be made welcome.

Gwen Ingham had a strong personality and commanding voice; she was outspoken and much of her conversation was characterised by a raw and dry sense of humour. She was also a fine looking woman especially in her twenties and thirties – as many of the village photographs testify. Friends came to see her from far and wide. Her house and shop were a haven of sociability and on an average day endless pots of tea would be dispensed, each specially made for the visitor of the moment and often accompanied by home made bread and cakes. At least that was usually the situation, but there were odd days when she would be exceptionally busy or getting ready to go out. On these occasions approaching visitors would be met with a tirade from deep within the house: "It's no use you coming here; I can't do with you today". On these rare instances discretion became the better part of valour and the hapless visitor was wise to retreat.

Gwen was born in No.2 Long Row in the village square in January 1921 the daughter of John and Gertrude Wyatt (nee Scotchbrook). Educated in the village school, she is depicted at the centre of a 1928 photograph of the school's twenty pupils. In the back row of the group is Bert Sheppards who also lived his entire life in the village.

On leaving school she worked in the South Wigston post office. She would cycle to Glen station and catch the train to Wigston. In 1938 she was crowned Newton Harcourt May Queen – a tradition in the village which survived until the 1950s. In April 1940 she married David Ingham at St Luke's Church.

Gwen at work in the Post Office in 1957.

IN MEMORY OF
GWEN INGHAM
1921 – 2004
LIFELONG RESIDENT OF NEWTON HARCOURT
FROM ALL HER FRIENDS IN THE VILLAGE

They were to have two children; Peter, who emigrated to Australia and Diana, who continues her association with Newton Harcourt.

In 1949 Gwen became sub-postmistress, moving from No.2 Short Row to the post office in School Lane. The shop also sold newspapers, shoe hardware, groceries and fruit and veg. Gwen delivered the newspapers in all weathers, often falling off her bike in icy conditions. The shop was a great convenience for the village in more ways than one as the "affairs of state" were avidly discussed within its diminutive portals. The shop was also welcome to passers by on the Grand Union canal but no profit was ever made. David would frequently say that it cost him ten pounds a week for Gwen to run the shop. The "tick" system was liberally applied and when the shop finally closed in 1981 Gwen was still owed money.

Although the shop had gone, visitors remained welcome. She regularly spread flowers from her garden to gardens throughout the village and parcels of daffodils were sent to relatives in Wales for St David's day. In January, her house became a marmalade factory producing a product in a class of its own whilst in November, if you took a basin, you got a Christmas pudding. Christmas saw a line of sausage rolls and minced pies which found their way into every corner of the village and far beyond. Even the village dogs and cats would not pass her gate until they had a biscuit or a saucer of milk. On Shrove Tuesdays, she ensured that all the village's elderly people had pancakes.

It was this role as carer that was perhaps Gwen's greatest attribute, as she devotedly nursed elderly aunts, mother and husband through their infirmities and final illnesses.

In 1988, Gwen was honoured by the Royal British Legion for her services to the Poppy Appeal. Six years later she was honoured by The Queen with an invitation to a royal garden party at Buckingham Palace in recognition of her services to the village. As the village's many visitors walk along the railway footpath they will pass the seat, placed by the Friends of Newton Harcourt, bearing an inscription of dedication to Gwen Ingham. Few will ever know the legend which lies behind her name. As a human being she was almost as perfect as it is possible to get.

The day before Lent is called Shrove Tuesday. This was always, until about 1960, an occasion for fancy dress, dancing, eating and drinking late into the night.

The wedding of David Ingham and Gwen Wyatt on 27 April 1940. The party are seen in Post Office Lane with the telephone box and Old Croft Farm visible in the background.

20th Centry Profile: Evelyn Gurney
Childhood memories of Newton Harcourt
(as told to her son, David)

"All of my childhood recollections are based on Newton Harcourt to which we went in 1917, when I was three. We lived at the top of the village in a tied cottage which belonged to farmer Hirst, for whom dad was working. There were four of us in the cottage; mum dad, myself and my sister Ellen, who was soon to start work. Sister Elsie was away from home in service somewhere. At first I scarcely knew my brother Charles. He'd gone off to war soon after my second birthday, before we moved to Newton. Nearly a year later came the news that he'd become one of the casualties from the Western Front. He'd been wounded in the leg and needed an immediate operation; he also caught pneumonia and spent a long time recovering in a London hospital before he was fit to come home on leave. He came back to a house and village that he'd not seen before. By then I was still less than four years old and he was almost 22, so it wasn't surprising that he seemed more like an uncle than a brother. He brought me a doll but my mother said I was too young for it and put it away in a box. Some years later we went to look for it but it had rotted and it fell apart; it broke my heart.

I have good memories of my years in Newton Harcourt. My dad was usually out working around the farm or in the fields, sometimes he would be sheep shearing, sometimes hedge laying. My mother and I would take things to him but what I liked best was when she and I walked alongside the stream and took our tea by the waterfall. The stream usually flowed quite gently in the summer but had cut a deep bed where it wound its way through the fields. We eventually found out it was called the River Sence; after that, when it flooded, we called it the River Nonsence. The fields and roads were sometimes very deeply covered; I remember the baker coming from Kilby with his horse's belly touching the water. St Luke's was our village church but the minister only came once in three weeks so that he could also hold services in Wistow and Kilby. When we went to the service in Kilby there were quite a procession of villagers going in that direction. I loved to see our church decorated for the harvest festival. On the day after, it would be Dad's job to take the flowers to the hospital in Leicester. It was quite a long trek for the horse and cart.

Winters could be long and cold. It was usual to see the canal frozen over and one year it was so cold that the lake at Wistow Hall was frozen solid. It was a rare and memorable sight to see the skaters on it. When I was eleven, my brother Charles married Doris Blackwell and sister Elsie married Albert Dilkes. By accident the two weddings had been arranged on the same day. We all went to Elsie's wedding in the village but I was sorry that we weren't able to go to Charles's.

All of Newton's children went to the village school which was situated close to the railway cutting. The school mistress came from Kilby. Of the village children I recall the Scotchbrooks, Walter Tyrell and Gwen Wyatt who was five years younger than I was. I became the first child from the village to pass the scholarship examination and was then sent to Wyggeston Girls School in Leicester. It was a difficult time especially in Winter. I could see trains from my bedroom window but the station itself was too far away for my liking. It was not too bad when I could cross the fields but that depended on the light and good weather. Once when I was on the field path I disturbed a snake; it was probably a grass snake but it scared me enough. My dad usually met me in the winter but there was the prize giving day when he expected me on the later train but I managed to catch the one before. There was no one at the station so I set off very apprehensively in the dark. I got frightened when I heard someone walking towards me; it was a neighbour who offered to walk back with me but I was still scared and ran the rest of the way home to the cottage.

I left school when I was fourteen bothered that my parents could ill afford the expense. The year before I left was the one in which a plane crashed near the village. Charles and Doris had come to visit that day and we were all watching the plane; it was usually so quiet that the rare noise of the plane was enough to attract anyone's attention. This one had circled around and flew low towards Great Glen; we heard the crash and rushed down the hill to see the plane on fire. The pilot had no chance to survive and was later buried in

Evelyn with her mother. Newton Harcourt in the early 1930s.

the churchyard. Years later a very elegant headstone appeared. One other gravestone always attracted my attention. It was in the shape of a church and marked the grave of a boy I had been at school with; he died of scarlet fever when he was eight.

My first job was at Ludlam's grocers in Wigston; I served in the shop which was situated at the end of Newton Lane opposite a butchers shop where pigs were sometimes killed. I was only a few miles away from home but I lived at the shop because it had an off license which stayed open late so it was not easy for me to get home."

Evelyn later married, moved to Rugby in 1939 and eventually became a post mistress. Her mother died in 1942.

The following extracts are from the second part of her story.

"After Mum died, Dad was living alone in his cottage and it wasn't easy for me to visit him from over twenty miles away. I can remember cycling there with cousin Ernie from Hillmorton; it was quite a struggle for both of us. I wasn't used to cycling any distance and Ernie was a bit on the heavy side. I can see him now, legs up and down, going at one speed, never hurrying. When we finally got back to our house I asked him if he wanted to stop for a drink but he said 'If I get off this bike now I won't be able to get on again'. It was much easier when we could go to Dad's by car and take a few things to him. When we got near to the village I would be looking out for the blind man who always opened the gate across the narrow road from Wistow into Newton Harcourt. He was another Ernie; Ernie Bird from Fleckney. He had been attending to that gate for years and would take pleasure in recognising my voice. It being Sunday we would usually find Dad working in his vegetable garden. He would be thrilled to see his grandchildren and they were always intrigued to see the cottage. After a while we would all take a walk down the lane, over the railway bridge then along the canal to the lock keepers house. The children liked to climb on the lock gates, cross over the canal to the other side then walk along the path through the spinney. On the way back we could walk along the small path by the railway, past the school house that I remembered

so well. Sometimes a long train would rattle past; if we were quick enough we could count the wagons."

Evelyn's father died in 1948 but until a few years before her own death in 2004 she continued to visit the village whenever she had an opportunity. We were able to scatter her ashes in the churchyard where her parents had been laid to rest in unmarked graves.

20th century profile: Jan Grzyb
by Colin Garratt

Jan Grzyb brought the real horrors of World War Two to Newton Harcourt. A white Russian from north eastern Poland, he was born in 1922 into a farming family but apparently ran away to join the Polish army in 1938. The German invasion the following year saw Jan join the Polish resistance which, in common with other movements in German occupied countries, was met with vicious reprisals. It would appear that his service in this guise was exemplary as he was to leave the war with medals including, it is believed, the St George Cross. Jan and a group of resistance fighters were eventually captured by the Germans and he was to witness at first hand his colleagues being hung and burnt alive in war crimes too heinous to describe. It is not known how he avoided being killed but he became a chauffeur to the German SS. He was eventually captured by the allies and wearing German uniform, became a prisoner of war and was sent to a POW camp on the Isle of Wight.

Jan Grzyb was typical of the thousands of displaced persons all over Europe following World War 2. Jan was both wounded and heavily traumatised by his war time experiences becoming a shadow of the man he had once been. However, this didn't prevent him from marrying an English girl named Hazel Jupe whilst on the Isle of Wight. A job was eventually found for him on a farm at Illston in Leicestershire. A later job was taken at Wistow Grange working for Edgar Smart's brother the death of whom led to him coming to Newton Harcourt in 1960 to work for Edgar.

The family lived at No.7 Long Row, a small cottage adjacent to Elms Farm. The marriage was to yield eight children; three boys

Jan Grzyb in the piggery. Some of Edar Smart's derelict farm machinery is visible in the background.

Jan in Poland in the 1930s before the war tore his life apart.

41

Above: The Grzyb family at Newton Harcourt in the mid 1960s. Left to right front row: Nina, Susan, Sheila, Hazel, Jan, Angie, Maggie, Mitch. Back row: Victor and Roger.

Right page: The funeral procesion arrives at Newton Harcourt churchyard: the final resting place of Jan and Hazel. This was the first horsedrawn funeral in Newton Harcourt for sixty years.

and five girls. They had an extremely strong family identity with high cheek bones giving them a classic Slavonic appearance.

In 1983, I was accompanied by my then partner Maggie Grzyb on a "Last Steam Locomotives" expedition to north eastern Poland. We were searching the forests around Czarna Bialostocka close to the Russian border for German military engines left from World War One and we saw a man outwardly identical to Jan in facial features, height, stance, build, posture and clothes. It was an eerie experience.

Despite having such a wonderful family, Jan's wartime scars never left him and he eventually destroyed all his medals. He was irascible and became a master of invective, peevishly referring to Hazel as "Babushka"(Old woman), whilst there were no female misdemeanours which could not be satisfactorily corrected by a good spanking.

Influenced by Edgar Smart, Jan kept pigs and built a piggery in Edgar's meadow immediately next to the bridleway leading from the village square and he eventually left No.7, having nominally divorced Hazel, to set up home in a wooden hut next to the piggery. He also kept free range chickens and the eggs produced became fabled; I have never tasted any to compare; they were large and fresh with hard dark brown shells and bursting with flavour. This piggery abode was charmingly rustic. A small stream meandered its way alongside whilst all around lay farm machinery discarded by Edgar Smart over many years. The machines stood alongside elm trees and tall rambling blackberry bearing hedges like sculptures.

Jan lived contentedly in the piggery until the death of Edgar Smart when he had to vacate the land. Whereupon he moved the wooden hut from the meadow to the bottom of the garden at No.7. In recompense for what he had lost in the field he created a thriving vegetable garden in the grass verge alongside the main road and those who had good relations with him would be the proud recipients of some true country produce.

Jan liked a drink and one of the enduring aspects of village life was a shadowy figure, with a half drunk bottle of liquor protruding from his pocket, rolling along the Long Row around midnight singing loudly to his heart's content. On such occasions he would be the happiest man in the parish but the occupants of No.7 would batten down the hatches locking all doors and putting out the lights – ever fearful of his drunken presence.

Newton Harcourt lost its most colourful character when Jan died in a road accident in 1997, only two days after Hazel's death from a heart attack. The joint funeral which this amazing family organised for their mother and father is evidenced in the adjacent picture. It is fitting that three houses in Newton Harcourt continue to be occupied by members of the Grzyb family over half a century after Jan and Hazel arrived in the village.

Village Life
(As told by Margaret Jewal)

I was born in a small farming village in Leicestershire in the year 1922. I was the ninth of 13 children. We lived in a 4 bedroom cottage with a 'living room', a 'parlour' and a 'scullery'. Fresh water for drinking had to be fetched in buckets from the village pump. Rain water was used for washing the clothes and was collected in a water-butt. Our lighting was from a large lamp which was filled with oil – the top having a burner and a wick which was lighted and controlled by turning the wick 'up or down' with the means of a turnable handle. There was no electricity until I was 15 years old (1937).

By the time I reached the age of 8 years, my older sisters were quite grown up and were responsible for the well-being of the younger children, washing, dressing etc… Our family, like others in the village was very closely knit and we learned the art of 'sharing' at an early age. Life was hardy rather than hard.

Our tiny school was for children aged between 5 and 11 years. The school consisted of one large classroom with a raised platform at one end which doubled as a stage, plus library. In the classroom were desks to seat a maximum of 20 children (our register quoted the number attending in 1930 as 12). There was a blackboard and easel, Teacher Table (desk), a large cupboard containing books and facing the class in the centre wall a huge open fireplace surrounded by a guard.

School began at 9 am with half an hour playtime at 10:30 am to 11 am and dinner break from 12 mid-day till afternoon lessons which were 1:30 pm to 3pm. They were happy days with a variety of Teachers – all were motherly, caring for the individual as well as administering a necessary amount of discipline. The main lessons taught were reading, writing and arithmetic. Learning to spell correctly was essential – this was taught by splitting each word and sounding each syllable i.e. cor..rect..ly. The alphabet was recited by the class each morning until firmly imprinted in the mind. Letters were put together to form words i.e. AT BAT CAT (a simple way of forming words)

Multiplication tables were taught in much the same way, by reciting (again quite simple). Apart from the 3 R's we were taught English, History and acquired a basic knowledge of the Geography of the 'British Isles' and Dominions. We enjoyed singing 'Patriotic Songs' and English Folk songs. Girls were also taught to sew – to make pinafores or simple dresses, also to knit fine lace and woollen socks. Boys learned to cultivate small plots of ground and also did some handicraft work, 'we didn't have calculators or computers in those days!' we were taught instead to use our minds and hands.

A uniform was not necessary for my infant schooling

Above: Folk dancing in the Square, circa 1933.

Left page: Louise Scotchbrook delivering mail, No. 1 Long Row in the background.

– but we wore much the same dress which was warm and hard wearing. Thick dresses for the girls over which we wore a nice clean white pinafore – our long stockings and knickers were woollen and a pair of button sided boots made up our winter clothing. Summer wear was light and brighter – cotton dresses and leather type sandals or shoes.

"One never attended school without a clean 'hankie' usually kept safe by a safety pin attached to one pinafore". Boys wore breeches during the summer. Coats were for most children 'hand-me downs' from older brother or sister. On cold mornings – mothers would often appear at play-time with cans of hot cocoa for all.

After school register had been read and all children accounted for, a prayer was said and we sang a hymn. At the end of the close of our school day another prayer would be said before dismissal.

The church and Sunday school played a large and essential part in our education, religious instruction was given also by the Vicar who would come for one hour each week to tell us stories from the Bible and test our knowledge.

After School

Even at the early age of 8 – children had certain commitments in the home especially where there was a large family – my daily task was to take my duster and clean off all dust from the furniture – also to dry the dishes and help feed the chickens – (which most people kept in those days). Because I was lucky enough to live in a village surrounded by woods and meadows – there wasn't a need to look far for somewhere to play.

During the summer and after the jobs around the home had been attended to – we would make for the fields, building dens, dressing our dolls in daisy chains and sharing a 'make-believe' world . The long holiday was spent barefoot in the hay fields or fishing the streams armed with a jam jar dangling from a piece of string or, a stick with a string attached on the end a bent pin for a hook.

Above: *The Newton Harcourt Women's Institute has been an enduring aspect of village life for almost a century. Meetings have always been held on the second Tuesday of each month – a tradition that continues to this day. In November 2012 the organization's 26 members will celebrate its 90th anniversary. As might be expected the WI activities over the years have been legion. Some years ago members took part in a Churchyard Survey organized by Leicestershire and Rutland Federation of WI. All the graves in Wistow and Newton Harcourt Churchyards were recorded in detail. This information is now in the Records Office in Wigston. Similarly a Field Survey was carried out a few years later.*

Left page: *A Wistow Estate tractor, perhaps their first, possibly just north of the village in about 1920. It is an International model 8-16 Junior. This tractor had a reputation for ruggedness and smooth running. Behind it is an impressive plough, showing the revolution that came with mechanised farming.*

It was especially fun to rise at first light on a misty September morning – don our wellies and armed with a large basket would try to race the herdsman for the first mushrooms. With a full basket we'd run home and each armed with a knife would peel the mushrooms for breakfast before going off to school. This was a great treat as our normal breakfast was either porridge or toast and dripping. Other cereals were too scarce and too costly.

Village roadways were quite narrow in 1930 – Motor cars were rarely seen and most people had to rely on their two legs or, if lucky enough to acquire one 'the bicycle'. Visitors to the villages were rare except for the essentials. Early morning saw the milk lorry arrive to collect the churns of new milk from the local farms. Mid-week brought the hardware van with its collection of pots, pans, clothes pegs, oil for the lamps and the news of the week! The driver heralded his arrival by clanging a metal strip against a basin. Saturday evening was the butchers van and the green grocers van. Monkey nuts (peanuts) were 1 penny a bag.

Winter was early to bed – usually 6 pm – the evenings long, dark and cold. As I got older I was allowed to stay up an extra hour to listen to the wireless – a primitive contraption by today's standards, which consisted of a speaker attached to an accumulator by which it worked. There was one station but this was mostly entertainment with plenty of light comedy. Other winter pass time-times included board games, such as 'Drafts', 'Snakes and Ladders', also the gramophone (not like today's record player). We read lots of books, told stories and sang around the piano.

Monday evening was an exception I belonged to the local 'Brownie' group – we would meet from 6 pm to 7:30 pm for various activities which 'Brownies' do! – Games, Folk dancing, Tying knots, learning the Morse-code, House wifery and the rudiments of self-preservation.

Christmas was a wonderfully exiting time – Carol singing with the church choir and mince-pies at the 'Manor'. A visit to Santa in his grotto and digging for a pressie. A visit to the Pantomime was a day to remember, Teacher would ask, "all those going to the Pantomime to stand". Everyone stood of course, so school was then closed for the day. The Annual Christmas Treat was another happy occasion – armed with mug and spoon we headed for the village hall for jelly, iced bun and lemonade, Lots of games, and a present from under the Christmas tree.

Mid-Summer was time for outdoor activities , such as the village fete with organised games, such as 'rounders', the obstacle race, 'Tug of War' and lots more. A summer highlight was a trip to skeggie (Skegness). Mum with dress tucked in large striped bloomers paddling in the sea, sticky rock, a bag of shrimps, the Punch and Judy, AND Donkey rides, Oh! Such Fun!" Then the ride home in the 'Charabanc' (a kind of large comfortable bus).

Then there was 'Empire Day' (now long forgotten), children dressed in the National costumes of the then 'British Empire' would ride on the gaily trimmed hay wagon. There was great 'National' pride in the dancing and singing.

The 1st Day of May was a joyful occasion – trimming the Maypole (a pole with hoops, trimmed with flowers and ribbons) which was then carried round the village accompanied by girls in pretty dresses, boys in neat white smocks (or shirts) and singing the songs which their mothers sang before them, of the new life in the trees and flowers. There was dancing – the Jester on his hobby-horse making everyone laugh.

Life was never dull, never boring, childhood meant accepting our parents teaching, learning to respect each other, to give and appreciate all that we received. To give an impression that we were never 'naughty' would be truly wrong. It is natural instinct of children to exercise self-expression and show an eagerness for independence. Sometimes, we find it difficult to accept wise counselling.

I was often punished, sometimes I thought 'unfairly' – but, with each year we grow a little wiser and eventually are able to except that in life there must be rules. "To be able to give an order we must also be willing to accept an order. Old fashioned values maybe! True nevertheless."

Getting in the coal at No. 2 Long Row. Left to right: Gertrude Wyatt (Gwen's mother), John Gardener, Joyce Bent and Gwen circa 1930.

Gwen Wyatt as May Queen in Post Office garden 1938.

Canal

By Joe Goddard

The canal at Newton Harcourt winds through the south side of the parish, a haven of peace that mirrors the reedy stillness of its embankments. It benignly overlooks the ancient landscape of ridge and furrow, woodland and floodplain to the south of it, and enriches the village some fifty yards to its north, with the calls of water birds and the pleasant commotion of boats passing through the locks on the climb south, or as they descend towards Leicester.

The canal is in fact an important part of the national network. It is the main east link joining the River Trent and the great northern canal ways such as the Trent and Mersey, and even the North Sea, to the main southern artery the Grand Junction Canal with its many offshoots such as the Oxford and the Coventry canals, the Birmingham system (with more canals than Venice) and all points south to London and thence to the Thames Estuary or Bath.

At Newton it rises through three pairs of locks to just over three hundred feet above sea level. Because of this importance as a central link, the canal is always busy in the summer these days, with a boat coming through every few minutes and other boats moored up for the night or a day or two, to taste the peace and take in the splendid view, especially looking south across the Sence Valley.

It was once very different. The canal, (or 'the Cut' as it is still called) was the result of much wrangling and confusion when, by private Act of Parliament, it was imposed in 1793 upon a still largely feudal countryside. Although the upheaval of field enclosure had already changed the pattern of farmland for good, the relationship of landlord and tenant remained medieval. The canal was an aggressive sinew of the new industrialising England, carrying goods, especially coal and granite through this Arcadian world, to London. The boat people were notoriously a law unto themselves and not at all above taking the Lord of the Manor's game to improve the diet on their boats. Not surprisingly most local landowners fought the canals bitterly. At Wistow the Earl of Denbigh (married to the widow of a Halford family landowner) raised every possible objection but quietly over-subscribed for landowner's shares when he saw the cause was lost. He also decreed that the towpath, which follows the canal's right-hand side for nearly all its fifty-two miles from Leicester, southwards towards Norton

The canal and its charms are an important part of village life.

Junction, in Northamptonshire, should change sides where it met the Wistow estate at Turnover Bridge near Kilby and run on the left side as far as Kibworth Bridge, thus putting the canal between the towpath and its boatmen, and the Wistow Estate.

Our canal, 'The Leicester Line', is made up of two canals, the Leicestershire and Northamptonshire Union, ('the LNU') from Leicester to Market Harborough and the original Grand Union Canal ('the GUC') which joined the LNU at Foxton and linked it to the main London - Birmingham Canal, the Grand Junction, at Norton Junction. The canal was originally called the Navigation and the men constructing it were called "navigators" or "navvies".

The excavation and making of the canal were, by the standards of the eighteenth century, astronomically expensive. The subscription raised 'to extend the navigation from Leicester to Market Harborough' amounted to £29,600 – millions in today's money. Beginning at West Bridge, Leicester, it would use the River Soar as far as Aylestone Meadows, then (parting company from the Soar and becoming a "proper canal") passing through Kilby Bridge, Newton Harcourt and past Fleckney and Saddington to Market Harborough

and Northampton. However, funds had run out by 1809 when the canal arrived at Debdale near Smeaton Westerby, having passed through Newton in 1795.

The canal's arrival in the Newton area had been stormy. From its foundation in 1793 the LNU's finances were sketchy and stretched to extremes. At one stage canal bridges and lock houses were sitting, completed, in the open countryside (their contractors

had been paid) awaiting the arrival of the canal (whose contractors had not). By March 1795 the work had reached the parish. It was at this point the "Great Riot" broke out – the biggest incident in the two canals' construction. It seems that the outbreak began when two drunken navvies (canal-diggers) assaulted a shopkeeper in Kibworth Beauchamp. They were arrested and taken to Leicester for trial, escorted by about forty "fencibles" (part-time militia) on 30th March. On route, the column was ambushed and the prisoners were freed by "at least threescore" (60) of their comrades. The Leicester magistrates immediately sent the Loyal Leicester Volunteer Infantry and the volunteer cavalry. The cavalry came straight to Newton where they found and arrested "four of the most desperate of the rioters" in the Bull Inn – now Sycamore House – in the village square. The following day they captured another nine

Above: A steamer and butty approaching Bridge 79 (High Bridge) from Kibworth. Watercolour by Margaret Jessica Goddard, 1898.

Left page: Wistow Church slumbers on a summer's afternoon as we look through canal bridge number 79, which has always been called High Bridge because of its views over the Sence Valley.

rioters including the notorious "Red Jack" and "Northamptonshire Tom" who had "terrorised every county they have resided in." Most were in fact acquitted but a couple of them were offered the interesting choice of going to gaol or joining the navy.

The canal could not proceed through Market Harborough owing to the hostility of the Paget family, local squires and landowners. Instead, it was forced to climb the hill by Foxton through a dramatic "flight" of 10 locks. The lock chambers on this famous construction were compelled by financial constraints to be of "narrow canal" width – seven feet wide at lock chambers. This, and the corresponding narrow flight at Watford twenty-two miles south at the other end of this "summit level", determined the

character and the future of the 'Leicester Line'. It would always be a narrow canal and a commercial poor relation of the Grand Junction despite its geographical importance.

The canal reached the Grand Junction Canal at Norton Junction in 1813 and trade prospered for some time, particularly in the Leicester Line's staple cargoes of coal and granite and also iron, and pottery and lime. Rough granite blocks, to be found all over the older parts of Newton, were probably brought by boat in about 1830.

However, from the 1860s the railway made increasing inroads into the canal's business and it is clear from canal company correspondence that a decreasing income was forcing economies in maintenance by the 1890's. Joshua Fellows of the canal haulage firm Fellows Morton and Clayton pressured the management to widen the locks at Foxton and Watford – in 1900 this resulted in the Foxton Inclined Plane, a mechanical wonder of the canal world. However

the canal still did not prosper. The Inclined Plane was considered too expensive to run and was taken out of service in 1910. All canals came under government control in the First World War, when traffic and revenue improved. This improvement continued into the early 1920s, although the canal was moribund when the Second World War arrived. This time the canal was brought back to a feeble flicker of life for a few years. Three writers have left haunting descriptions of the Leicester Line at that time. L.T.C. Rolt in his book "Narrowboat" describes his travels in 1939 on "the lost and lovely waterway" where the Harborough arm was so weed choked as to be scarcely navigable, and he writes of "the sylvan beauties of Newton Harcourt". The second writer, Susan Woolfit wrote of her experiences as a war worker boatwoman in "Idle Women" (1947). She describes the canal as a narrow channel in the middle of a mass of weed. Phillip Stevens, in his book "The Leicester Line" (1972) describes the canal in the war years as "a stretch of tranquil beauty in a maniac world, with rarely a boat to be seen".

Above: Newton Lock Cottage. Apart from the supply of mains water in the 1950s, this house remained unchanged from 1795 until 2005 when a separate wing was added, doubling it in size.

Left page: Newton Harcourt Lock House. L to R back row: Jack, Ann, Harold, Joseph Faulkner.
Front row: Ted, Mrs Faulkner Senior, Emily and Frank.

By 1950 traffic had again dwindled, and the canal was choked with weed except for a navigable channel down its centre. The towpath was a sea of cow parsley. However in that year the first ever Inland Waterways Association Boat Rally was held at Market Harborough Basin. This marked the beginning of the national campaign to cherish our canal system. But the immediate position of the Leicester Line was not good: there was even a move to fill it in and use it as a bus route. At one stage a cement mixer tipping wheel was used to move the rotting paddles in Newton Top Lock. The canal was probably saved by the presence of three big reservoirs on its summit (Foxton-Watford) section which could provide plenty of water to both north and south.

But in the early 1960s there was increased interest in our national canal heritage. The Inland Waterways Association became a popular institution and our canals began to be dredged and cleared of weed. The pioneering Foxton Boat Services began business in the middle of the decade and boat traffic through Newton gradually began – one or two boats a month to begin with, still finding the canal an adventure with weed, leaks and jammed lock gates. However, by the 1980s the canal was as we see it today – except today there are more boats and more walkers.

As a linear nature reserve it enables a whole range of birds, mammals, fish and insects to travel long distances in security from one wooded area to another, to delight the eye of boaters and walkers alike. In fact, the ten mile stretch between Kilby (Turnover Bridge) and Foxton Locks forms one of the longest "Sites of Special Scientific Interest" in Britain.

As a walkers' paradise the towpath can have few rivals, running as it does in its own environment of trees, flowers, grass and rushes. Newton Top Lock is a particularly good starting point: you can make your walk as long as you like (to London in one direction or the northern Pennines in the other). Why not try the two and a half mile towpath walk to Kilby Bridge, with its excellent pub The Navigation, with liquid refreshment of course, and very good food... Also, walking south from Newton (joining the canal at Top Lock or at Manor Bridge (Bridge 80), after a few hundred yards you pass under High Bridge (Bridge 79), and immediately to the unspoilt and breathtaking view across the Sence Valley, taking in fields, woods and Wistow Church, the site of the martyrdom of Prince Wistan of Mercia (later Saint Wistan) in 849AD. If you continue you will walk through miles of unspoilt countryside, the peace punctuated only by occasional passing trains.

Above: Newton Top Lock and Lock Cottage, a tranquil scene often enlivened by passing narrow boats.

Left page: Grand Junction Canal Company's mileposts located on the section between Newton Harcourt and Turnover Bridge.

Left page: Newton Top Lock – a place of many reflections.

Above: The canal in winter represents another of Newton Harcourt's charms and skating on the ice has always been a popular and much looked forward to activity with the village children. It was however a very different situation for the canal boat operators as all movements came to a standstill and commodities were delivered late and during extreme winters seriously so. Severe winters and dry summers, leading to insufficient water, were occupational hazards which rendered the canal system at a great disadvantage compared with its great competitor the railway.

Railway

By Colin Garratt

The Industrial Revolution made its mark on Newton Harcourt in two dramatic ways, although the sylvan beauty of the village remained un-affected. First came the canal in 1795 and sixty two years later the Midland Railway's new route to London. The railway was a far brasher symbol of the Industrial Revolution than the canal had been but instead of desecrating the environment - as Ruskin and Wordsworth would have had us believe – it made a sublime contrast with nature. The railway – and the canal – made Newton Harcourt more interesting and more beautiful.

The Midland Railway was formed in 1844 by the amalgamation of several companies which saw Leicester connected with Derby, Chesterfield, Sheffield and Leeds, whilst shortly afterwards Derby was linked to Manchester. It was essential that these industrial towns were connected with the capital and the Midland Railway achieved this by the line from Leicester to Rugby, via Wigston and Countesthorpe, which had opened in 1840 as part of the Midland Counties Railway. Upon reaching Rugby the Midland continued over the London and Birmingham Railway to London Euston (the present day West Coast Main Line). The massive increase in traffic as the Industrial Revolution developed made the arrangement with the London and Birmingham Railway increasingly untenable and the Midland built a line south from Wigston to Hitchin via Market Harborough, Desborough, Kettering, Wellingborough and Bedford. This brought the railway to Newton Harcourt. From Hitchin the Midland Railway's trains ran to London over the metals of the Great Northern Main Line to London Kings Cross (the present day East Coast Main Line). The first train ran

through Newton Harcourt in 1857 and local stations were built at Wigston Magna, Great Glen, Kibworth and East Langton.

Inevitably, the Midland Railway's trains played second fiddle to the Great Northern's and this arrangement soon became as unsustainable as had been the one with the London and Birmingham. The solution was for the Midland to build its own route to London extending southwards from Bedford through Luton and St Albans to London St Pancras. The Midland Railway's arrival in the capital was celebrated by the magnificence of St Pancras station and the Grand Hotel. Designed to outshine the adjacent terminals of Kings Cross and Euston. The architect was Sir George Gilbert Scott, who created a neo Gothic masterpiece. The station's roof span was the largest in Britain and the combined station and hotel became one of London's most magnificent buildings and one of the world's great stations. The first direct train from St Pancras passed through Newton Harcourt in 1868.

Newton Harcourt lies 6½ miles south of Leicester and southbound trains face a climb which begins at Kilby Bridge and continues through to Kibworth. One of Newton Harcourt's oldest residents, Bert Sheppards, who spent his entire working life at Elms Farm recalled coal trains stalling in the area of the village necessitating an assisting engine to be sent from Wigston. Although the Midand Main Line runs north to south, the section through Newton Harcourt makes an east west orientation – the only point between Leicester and London that this occurs. The Midland was one of Britain's largest railway companies. Their headquarters and works were at Derby which became

The world's most famous steam locomotive at Newton Harcourt. 'Flying Scotsman', working a Railway Correspondence and Travel Society special, following the end of steam working on the Midland Main Line. The thoroughbred is caught passing beneath the bridge on the Wigston to Fleckney road.

one of Britain's historic Railway Towns. Newton Harcourt was to witness an amazing variety of trains. From the mid 19th century the locomotives of Matthew Kirtley predominated; his ubiquitous double framed 0-6-0s handled freight traffic whilst passenger trains were operated by his 2-2-2s and 2-4-0s. Upon Kirtley's death in 1873 Samuel Johnson became Chief Mechanical Engineer and in 1883 the Midland adopted its glorious crimson lake livery. Johnson became famous for his beautiful 4-2-2 Spinners with 7' 9½" diameter driving wheels and also his three cylinder compound 4-4-0s. The company had a small engine policy and double heading of locomotives on both passenger and freight trains was commonplace. The Midland Railway introduced the first Pullman coaches, including sleeping cars and was one of the first to provide on-board dining facilities.

The Midland Railway survived until 1923 when Britain's 120 private railway companies were grouped together into four large organisations; the London Midland & Scottish(LMS), London North Eastern Railway(LNER), Great Western Railway(GWR) and Southern Railway(SR). The Midland was one of the constituents of the LMS and for some years the compounds and various classes of 0-6-0s continued, augmented by the mighty Garratt 2-6-6-2s, built for the LMS by Beyer Peacock of Manchester. But the accession of William Stanier as the LMS's Chief Mechanical Engineer in 1933 precipitated a mighty re-stocking of the motive power. The old and by then under powered designs of 19th century origin were progressively downgraded by such superb designs as the famous Black 5 4-6-0s for mixed traffic work, Jubilee 4-6-0s for express passenger operation and the 8F 2-8-0s for heavy freight.

I discovered Newton Harcourt one summer afternoon after school in the late 1940s when a friend suggested a bike ride. We set out from Oadby heading south and continued along the muddy quagmire known as "The Mere", which brought us out on the Wigston to Fleckney road close to Highfield House. Turning towards Fleckney we soon came to a railway bridge and leaning our bikes against the brickwork, stood on the cross bars and gazed onto the shining track. I willed a train to pass and soon a

Leicester's ex Midland Railway 2F 0-6-0 No.58298 was a regular engine on the Smelly Bone train. 15c was the code for Leicester (Midland) Motive Power Depot.

Jubilee Class 4-6-0 No.45685, 'Barfleur', heads a St Pancras to Bradford express train through Great Glen Station on 27 June 1959. 'Barfleur' was a Bristol engine for many years and their Jubilees were not normally seen through Newton Harcourt.

coal train came into sight and I clearly remember it to have been a Stanier 8F. The engine was making a superb roaring sound and pumping grey smoke into the air. Mesmerised I watched it approach until the engine's heavy exhaust beats became too frightening and we leapt from our crossbars. The smoke struck the bridge's underside and puthered up a mighty cloud. Another bridge was situated a quarter of a mile to the south and as we watched the engine forging its way towards it I wondered if the train would stretch between the two. To my sheer joy it did. The guard's van passing beneath our bridge as the engine's smoke hit the underside of the distant bridge in the heart of the village. Fear turned to wonder and that afternoon represented a turning point in my life. I returned to that magical spot on successive days and much of my remaining childhood was duly spent there watching ex Midland, LMS and British Railway's locomotives.

In those blissful pre - motorway years, a vehicle crossing the railway bridge on the Wigston to Fleckney road was an occasion. The railway was the pulse of the nation and a wonderful variety of trains could be seen carrying virtually every commodity imaginable. An endless succession of coal trains bound for London and the south from the pits of Nottinghamshire and Yorkshire; heavy rakes of iron ore being conveyed northwards from the Northamptonshire ironstone bed to the foundries of Nottinghamshire and South Yorkshire. Other commodities included steel, cement, oil, milk, fruit, vegetables, meat and other perishables, beer, cattle, mail and parcels – even pigeon specials taking thousands of homing birds to far away places for release. Most freights were long distance but some were local pick ups which called at intermediate stations like Great Glen and Kibworth to collect or set down wagons. Likewise the passenger trains were varied; locals, stopping at all stations including Leicester to Northampton trains, via Market Harborough or long distance expresses from St Pancras to Manchester or Leeds and Bradford and serving Leicester, Nottingham, Derby, Chesterfield and Sheffield. There were numerous "Reliefs" and "Specials" to support big events like major sporting fixtures or exhibitions. Movement of military personnel was also seen and these specials sometimes brought rare and unusual locomotives to Newton Harcourt. The most prestigious train of the day was the Thames Clyde Express making its four hundred mile journey from London to Glasgow. In contrast was the macabre "Smelly Bone", which took rotting cattle bones from the slaughter house at Freeman's Common to the glue factory near Market Harborough. The stench of rotting meat permeated the entire village as the superannuated former Midland Railway 0-6-0 trundled its hideous train of three wagons and a guard's van. The train always passed around lunch time and I remember

Above: Newton Harcourt bade farewell to its last steam trains in 1965, ending a tradition of 108 years. One of the last workings was the 14.35 freight from Leicester to Wellingborough, seen here passing milepost 92½ and approaching the village bridge. The engine is Stanier 8F 2-8-0 No.48670. The stately elm in the background is on Elms Farm and this tree was destined to die before the end of the century as a result of Dutch Elm Disease. Much of it was burnt as logs over succeeding winters at Elms Farm.

Left page: Newton Harcourt Signal Box was located immediately east of the railway bridge on the Wigston to Fleckney road. It was demolished during the 1930s. However, its location is still clearly in evidence. This picture, dated 1912, depicts a Down freight headed by Kirtley Double Framed 0-6-0 No.2552. This is almost certainly the only photograph of this signal box in existence.

refraining from eating my sandwiches until after "The Bone" had gone. Sometimes the wagons would stand in the sidings at East Langton for days before the contents were taken to the factory by which time the bones were alive with huge maggots.

In summer the railway embankments regularly caught fire from hot embers shot out of the locomotives. Often the blazes were furious and the village would be obliterated in smoke as it regularly was from the locomotives which issued a pungent smell of sulphur and oil which produced an elixir, especially when combined with the sweet smelling earth which seemed so peculiar to Newton Harcourt. There were many wonderful locomotives; the ex London & North Western "Super D" 0-8-0s with their offbeat rhythms and wheezing gasps reminiscent of a crying baby. They were the embodiment of the starkness of LNWR locomotive design and when heading south could be heard wheezing and slipping as they struggled to get their heavy freight trains on the move from Kilby Bridge.

Most of the express passenger trains were hauled by the beautiful Jubilees with their Brunswick Green livery, tapered boilers and brass nameplates which glinted in the sun. Their 6' 9" diameter driving wheels spinning sensuously. These engines had a wonderful syncopated three cylinder beat as they tackled the southbound climb through the village. Nationwide the class totalled 191 locomotives, some 50 of which were allocated to depots throughout the midland division; Kentish Town (London), Derby, Nottingham, Trafford Park (Manchester), Millhouses (Sheffield) and Holbeck(Leeds). The Jubilees had wonderful names commemorating great achievements in British history, including all our colonial possessions along with battleships, military and naval figures; Malta GC; Nigeria and Gold Coast were just three of the many fondly remembered names. Some expresses would be double headed by a Jubilee and a Compound, or a Black 5 and an ex Midland Railway's Simple 4-4-0. Trains were made up to whatever capacity was required – there was always an abundance of spare coaches in the sidings. If the train's weight exceeded the prescribed limit a pilot engine would invariably be attached.

The southbound expresses to London were followed by a stopping train, often headed by a former Midland Railway Compound 4-4-0 and standing on the village bridge on a damp summer evening, when the atmosphere was clear, it was possible to hear the Jubilee receding away to the south through Great Glen and simultaneously to hear the rhythmic throb of a Compound approaching Kilby Bridge from the north; the two, heard together, produced a mystical polyphony of six cylinders with tantalising cross rhythms; it was the most ecstatic music imaginable.

Summer days at the lineside were characterised by bottles of pop from the off licence in the village square – now Sycamore House – apple crush, dandelion and burdock or ice cream soda, made by Furnivals in neighbouring Fleckney. Once the pop had gone it was trips to the water pump in the village square, where the crystal clear water coming naturally chilled, gushed out endlessly. It had an earthy taste and a purity and was vastly superior to the bottles of spring water we buy today.

In the early 1950s most boys were interested in either the railways or football – or both. Train spotting was a national sport the excitement of which surpassed all superficial appearances. Britain had more than 25,000 main line steam locomotives and the object was to see them all. Only a tiny percentage of them could be seen at Newton Harcourt. There were hundreds of different designs. All reflected the history and development of the companies they originated from.

And so we sat on the banks at Newton Harcourt dreaming of rare locomotives. We particularly enjoyed the occasional rarity which passed en route to Derby Shops. These were engines begrimed and run down on their way to major overhauls at Derby Works. They would return weeks later issuing wafts of fresh paint across the embankments as they trundles past on rote to their home depots. They were known as 'shoppers'.

One particularly interesting train was the northbound milk empties from the express dairy at Cricklewood. This diagram used to pass around 4:30 in the afternoon and was capable of producing a whole range of motive power including occasionally

Autumn glory as a brace of Class 37 diesel electrics head a southbound aggregate train through the cutting with the Wigston to Fleckney road bridge in the background and milepost 92½ in the bottom right hand corner; a picture taken from the village bridge. Introduced in 1960, the Class 37s were one of the first generation of diesels which replaced steam. Over half a century later occasional examples could still be seen passing through Newton Harcourt.

a rare Jubilee.

The serious business of train spotting was not without some semblance of light relief. At the opposite end of the meadow adjacent to the village railway bridge was the canal lock house and there lived a girl a couple of years older than me named Mary Groom. She was beautiful, with golden plaits and would come up the field towards the railway bridge with a yoke and two buckets on her way to draw water from the pump in the village square. She looked exactly like the girl on the Kraft

Dairylea cheese wrapper. The moment I set eyes on her I would shout "Here comes Mary milkmaid the Dairylea girl". She was humourless and my jibes were guaranteed to create an angry reaction which was out of all proportion to the nature of the affront. She suffered my ribald taunts over 2 long summers until, one day, in a pique of temper, she attacked me and nearly succeeded in pushing me off the bridge. Occasional romps in the hayloft with a childhood sweetheart were too few; they, like the chugging barges carrying freight on the Grand Union canal, caused me to miss trains.

And when the long happy days at the lineside came to an end I would cycle back to Oadby along The Mere, having waited for the Burton to London beer trains. These were always worked by one of Burtons 'Crab' 2-6-0s which bought a delightful flavour of Lancashire and Yorkshire locomotive design practice to the Midland Main Line. My return home through the gathering twilight was observed by hooting shadowy owls and vast flocks of clamorous Rooks going to roost. I would always be black and sooty from having been around the railway all day. If my hair was washed in the sink the water would be black, as was the bath water, causing my mother to threaten that I would never be allowed near the railway again.

I did stay on a few occasions with the Harrop family whose house was alongside the water pump in the village square. They were a beautiful family; Cecil Harrop, the father, having once been a footman to the Goddard family at The Manor. I remember sitting up in bed late into the evening pooring over the engines I had seen that day and marking them in the wonderful Ian Allan ABC spotters' books. So potent was the magic of these little books that today, over sixty years later, they are still being published, albeit that they bear no relation whatsoever to what can be seen on the railway today – unbelievable!

These sojourns at the Harrops enabled me to listen to the rhythms of the railway throughout the night. It was as busy as by day, especially with heavy Toton to Brent coal hauls. Residents were frequently woken up by the deafening sound of these heavy trains struggling up the bank with flaming embers being shot from the locomotive's chimney. On still nights it was possible to hear the sounds of heavy shunting in the sidings at Wigston and even Knighton. The deep coughs of the locomotives, the spinning of wheels on a damp rail followed by the clanking of wagons; there is something deeply reassuring about falling to slumber to the sounds of steam locomotives shunting in the freight yard.

The passing of steam and the shift to a road based economy has rendered the railway a di smal shadow of its former magnificence with little to capture the imagination of the young. But there are times when the memories turn to dreams and the sounds of Newton Harcourt's romance with the age of steam are carried ghost like on the wind as it courses through the village amid the dark embrace of night.

Above: A southbound High Speed Train seen from the village bridge with the Wigston to Fleckney road bridge in the background and milepost 92½ in the bottom right hand corner.

Left page: Milepost 92½, located to the west of, and visible from, the village bridge, indicating the distance to London, St Pancras. Mileposts are located every quarter of a mile.

Elms Farm

By Colin Garratt

The village has five prominent farmhouses, administrative hubs of their little empires of fields and copses over the centuries. Of these, Hirsts Farm (also known as Poplars Farm) seems by far the oldest as it has a date stone inscribed 1714. The other farms, built later in the eighteenth or early nineteenth century, sit like anchored battleships amongst the lesser buildings.

Two of them, Old Croft Farm and Elms Farm, built around 1810/1812, are identical in many respects – they share the same tall, three storey slightly forbidding aspect and their brick is identical. Old Croft Farm has altered over the years, partly through foundation settlement and more recently through smartening but Elms Farm today is much as it was in the mid nineteenth century. It still sits, four square and brooding, looking across the fields as it stands at the western end of the village. It has out-

standing views for twenty or so miles around the Soar Valley to the north west and across the Sence Valley to Kilby and Foston to the south west.

It was a working farmhouse until 1985 and has the last remaining orchard within the village boundary. The last farming family at Elms were the Kennys – Joe and his son Wallace. Joe provided the two wheeled tumbrill or Honeypot to take away the contents of the toilet buckets ('nightsoil' it was called) from around the village and empty them in a small wood north of Newton. Long before that a dynasty called the Wards lived there and through incredible luck the different generations of the Wards can be seen in the following photographs from about 1880 to 1940 or so.

Charles Ward leading two horses and a well laden cart circa 1925.

Elms Farmhouse between 1905 and 1910, with John Ward's grandfather Charles Ward. Alongside him is one of the children's nursemaids.

The same view over a hundred years later with Colin Garratt's son James and daughter Marie-Louise emulating their forebears, by standing in the same positions. The lack of visible change enables us to take a long leap backwards into history.

John B. Ward has captioned this picture: 'A family group taken against the front entrance to the farmhouse, including my great grandfather Charles Bryan Ward, who owned the farm until his death in 1896, aged 50; my great grandmother, Elizabeth Ellen; and their children: my grandfather, his twin brother Joseph William, daughter May (who also died in 1896 aged 18) and three other young women, including a further daughter and Lucy Deacon, later to marry my grandfather. She was one of the Deacon family of clockmakers originating from Barton in the Beans.' It is a virtual certainty, judging by the apparent ages of the children, that this photograph was taken in 1895/6.

A hundred and fifteen years later the Garratt family assemble themselves in exactly the same position. The wooden porch has long since been taken down but its location is still clearly visible. On the front row are Colin Garratt's twin boys Anteaus and Dominion, who bring twins back to Elms Farm with three – year – old daughter Tamerlane, whilst behind are Colin Garratt's older children, James and Marie-Louise, and between them Colin and his Chinese wife Liu Yanchun.

Harvesting in the 1920s using a horse drawn reaper and binder.

John B. Ward's grandfather standing in front of the farmyard with the outbuildings in the background. This picture is likely to have been taken about 1915. The outbuildings have now been converted into dwellings.

The fecundity of nature. The two century old orchard at Elms Farm and Colin Garratt's daughter Tamerlane with one of the ancient trees. Summer 2010.

# Agricultural machinery of yesteryear

Seed drills for sewing wheat, oats or barley in straight lines in the fields. These examples were originally horsedrawn but were later adapted for tractors. Behind them stands a late nineteenth century farm wagon, and old style spades. Sheds around Newton were identical to this into the 1960s.

The process of 'threshing' seperates the harvested grain from the husks (called 'chaff'), the grain would then be sold. This picture shows threshing using a single cylinder traction engine – a 'farm engine' – to power the threshing machine (or 'drum') in the foreground. This would have been a familiar scene, and noise, around the village. Edgar Smart (farmer and agricultural contractor) replaced his traction engine in 1938, but threshing machines continued to make their distinctive hum until the late 1960s. The entire process of harvesting and threshing is now handled by the combine harvester. Interestingly, the modern 'combine' is far more wasteful of grain than a well-adjusted threshing machine.

The charm of any unspoilt farm. A miscellany of old farm machines. A 'tedder' lies in the foreground; this would have lifted the cut hay to let the air dry it.

In the foreground a horse–drawn and horse powered hay cutter.

Essential for making hay stacks (hay 'ricks') a hay 'elevator' powered by a Lister 'D' 1 ½ horsepower hopper cooled engine. You simply refilled the hopper with whatever liquid was available as the coolant boiled away.

St Lukes Church

By Joe Goddard

The Domesday Book in 1086 noted that among Newton's inhabitants there was a priest. This was unusual in a Leicestershire village. Was there already a church or chapel at Newton? At present we don't know, although we could argue that the church tower holds a clue to the church being of very ancient origin – Saxon or even Danish – we'll look at this later. Or perhaps the priest was the rector of Wistow, whose land included several acres at Newton in the late 13th century?

Wistow has been the mother church of Kilby and Newton – and of Fleckney until the 19th century – since at least 1220, when the rectory of Wistow was holding three services a week at Newton, including a chantry of Saint Leonard – a chantry was a kind of charity for the saying of prayers (in Latin, of course) for the dead.

The church today is a small simple building consisting, as you move from East to West, of chancel (the east end, separated from the rest of the church by a step), then the main body of the building, called the nave (where the congregation sit). Chancel and nave date from 1834, very plain and pleasing. Finally, at the west end, there's the simple sturdy stone tower,

which is all that is left of the older buildings on this site. The lower part of the tower dates from the late 13th century, but it uses round 'streambed' stones in a manner identical to that used for Tugby Church tower which is 10th century – Tugby Church was initiated by one Toki, a Viking – so Newton might arguably be of that period as well. The upper tower, of squared ironstone, is said to be 15th century, as are the doorway and lowest window, both in the west side of the tower. Inside the bell-chamber there are internal supports (or 'broaches'), which suggest that originally there was an intention to build a small spire on the tower – presumably the funds ran out before this was started.

The church building looks well cared for and its interior is airy, light and a pleasure to visit, but it has had a chequered history. For example in 1626 there was a complaint that the church door was broken down and the old style 'box' pews were 'rotten and decayed'. In 1777 more repairs were needed and in 1784 the seats were found to be 'beyond repair'. Finally in 1832 the rural archdeacon reported that the chancel and nave were 'falling to pieces', the pews so rotten and so thick

With its thirteenh century or earlier tower base and fourteenth century bell tower, St Luke's is a quintessential hamlet church.

with pigeon droppings that they could not be used. So in 1834 the church was rebuilt in the pleasant Georgian gothic style that we see today. It is much used, visited and loved. The single bell is now thought to be 15th century, so is one of the oldest in the county.

Another notable feature of St Luke's is the bullet-riddled weather vane. It jammed at some point in the 19th century and there was the problem of how to free it. The last Sir Henry Halford, a keen rifle shot, took aim from one of the bedroom windows in the Manor House, then peppered the weather vane until it started spinning again. It has given no more trouble from that day to this, though it does look like something from the wild west.

The churchyard was consecrated in 1875. With beautiful canal-side views over the fields and woods to the south east, and especially when carpeted in spring flowers, it is an enchanting spot.

There are one or two interesting headstones. You cannot miss the lovely miniature church over the grave of little Christopher Gardiner, who died in 1926 aged eight, of scarlet fever. The little monument was made by the boy's father, a stonemason. It was carved in the Long Row and brought to the churchyard in a wheelbarrow. The boy's father lies buried alongside. It was restored by Tom Snell of Newton and is visited from all over the country. Also look for the headstone of Henry Parsons, lock-keeper for 48 years, and of Flying Officer George Aldridge, who flew his RAF plane (a de Havilland 9A) into a tree while displaying his flying skills to his girlfriend near Great Glen.

There is another headstone, possibly unique in the whole country. This is the stone that marks the grave of a tramp and it is lettered, simply, 'IGNOTUS EX AQUIS ORA PRO ANIMA 28.V.1936.' – 'an unknown person taken from the water. Pray for his soul.'

The tramp had apparently had a stroke or heart attack early in the morning whilst shaving. He was using the canal as a mirror, and his belongings and shaving things were laid out

on the side at Newton Middle (Spinney) Lock.

Quite a few corpses used to be extracted from the canal at Newton – some suicides and some accidents and there was a set procedure for dealing with them all. When a body was reported in 'The Cut', the Great Glen policeman - in the 1920's and 30's his name was Tommy Steel - would chug up to Newton on his motorbike combination, with a stretcher and

Above: Newton Harcourt churchyard. Actually quite a 'young' churchyard, dating from 1875. The little church on the left is nationally famous. It marks the grave of Christopher Gardiner who died, aged 8, of scarlet fever in 1924.

Left page: St Luke's from the South East.

a grappling iron in the sidecar. The PC and a local volunteer would fish the corpse out with the grappling iron (which used to hang in the Old Forge at Great Glen). They would carry the body on the stretcher to Newton Top Lock Landing and up the field to Newton Square railway bridge. Then, either the corpse was placed in the little mortuary adjoining the village bakehouse and forge (all demolished now) beside the Square for collection for an inquest in Leicester, or the body was propped up in the sidecar and driven to Great Glen where the inquest was sometimes held.

They must have made a darkly comic pair: the immaculate policeman in his peaked cap on his polished motorbike, with his watery passenger lolling in the sidecar. On one occasion apparently they passed the bus from Glen at a point where in those days passing vehicles had to go slowly, and the bus visibly sank on its off-side springs as morbidly fascinated passengers pressed against the windows to have a look. No doubt PC Steel threw them a smart salute, as bike-combination police always did.

There is a well - attended service at St Luke's every third Sunday.

A slight relaxation from the twice - weekly services of medieval times before the chantry was suppressed by Elizibeth I, but this little church remains very much alive.

A particularly exciting event in the present church calendar is Harvest Festival which usually falls on St Luke's feast - day in early October. With sheaves of wheat, fruit, vegetables and flowers, and a considerable gathering of local people, the interior is not greatly different from the days of the Rev. Herbert Ransome ninety years ago.

The Christmas season at Newton begins in early December with a popular Carol Service followed by mince pies across the road at The Manor, courtesy of Anthony and Annette Goddard. The Midnight Mass on Christmas Eve night, when Christmas Day is welcomed in, is also a village event of beauty and joy engendering the true spirit of Christmas, and the church is always full.

Left page: Marriage of Margaret Jessica Goddard to Major John Aldridge, August 1899. Henry Langton Goddard, the brother of the bride, is in the middle of the group of three men by the church door. The happy couple are seen leaving the church after the ceremony. The one policeman on duty for crowd control was paid ten shillings.

This photograph of the church shows the simple 1834 interior.

Natural History of Newton Harcourt

By Colin Garratt

If we could turn the clock back sixty years and walk through the fields and bridleways around Newton Harcourt we would find a countryside teeming with life. Insects, birds, flowers – a Garden of Eden. Rambling overgrown hedges, ponds, ancient and stately trees, gurgling rivers; a beautiful, untidy landscape, tumbledown barns, old machinery, dead trees standing like sculptures and each a complete eco system of its own. A natural adventure playground for children with everything to nourish their imagination.

The lanes were quiet, there was little motor traffic and the peace and stillness amplified the sounds of the wild. Spring brought the mad March Hare and the dawn chorus which was deafening; it would wake you up and was equalled only by the clamour from the rookeries. In summer, the sonorous purr of turtle doves – summer visitors from Africa – provided an undertone to many species of song birds. A walk up the bridleway from the village square would reveal skylarks on all points of the compass. The birds seen as a distant speck, high above the ground, showered the earth with their rich bubbling music. There were yellowhammers, willow warblers, chiffchaffs, whitethroats, blackcaps and garden warblers to mention only a few. In contrast came the twilight hooting and screech of owls; droves of bats emerging from the woods, the churring of a grasshopper warbler, partridges calling across the darkening fields. moths, or fadges as we called them, swirled along the hedges and bridleways and intensified like driven snowflakes around any light.

The Grand Union canal had an eco system of its own; it was alive with water voles and moorhens whilst kingfishers were always in residence. Also in that aquatic wonderland were sedge and reed warblers whilst dragonflies and damselflies added a piquancy of their own.

On hot sunny days along the footpaths grasshoppers chirped in the verges and sprang around one's feet; butterflies were in abundance and diversity. Field mice and voles, frogs and grass snakes were frequently seen and every day would produce at least one enormous, intimidating bumble bee. Great Crested Newts flourished in the meandering water courses

Bee Orchids and other exotic wild flowers abounded in all their fragrant beauty and variety, as did blackberry bearing hedges; so many that pounds of the exotic fruit could be easily gathered on a short ramble. And the village was full of snails, thousands of them, which ensured an excellent population of song thrushes, one of the most beautiful songsters on the British list. Their beguiling rhythmic music would begin before dawn and with brief rest during the day, would continue tirelessly until darkness fell.

The winter calendar was little less dramatic, including

The Sence Brook at Manor Bridge looking towards Wistow.

huge flocks of lapwings, starlings in their thousands darkened the sky like a thunder cloud – one of the sublime sights of the wild. They would descend to roost in a coppice amid a babble of chatter audible almost a mile away. The mass of bodies huddled together would almost obliterate the trees from view. The following morning the trees and ground below would be white with their droppings. Rooks and jackdaws also consorted to form huge flocks. These itinerant birds would maraud querulously around one area for days and were a fine sight to behold as were the flocks of small birds searching for seeds; chaffinches, greenfinches and tree sparrows. A wild inheritance; our birthright.

This description of Newton Harcourt acts as a microcosm for the vast swathes of Britain's farmlands as they were in the 1970s but the creeping mass destruction to come was as unimaginable as it was pernicious. The ripping out of habitat, hedges, trees, woods and ponds on a massive scale and the widespread dowsing with chemicals has done irreparable

Above: One of G. K. Chesterton's "storehouse of sunsets" as Canada geese prepare to roost on Newton Harcourt's lake during one of the glorious sunsets of August 2011.

Left page: Thousands of starlings form a mushroom-shaped cloud as they prepare to roost at dusk. Flocks such as these are known as murmurations.

damage nationwide. Thousands of miles of hedgerow – the arteries of the wild – have been destroyed. The nightjar and the corncrake have long gone and many other creatures seem destined to follow their flight into oblivion.

All over Britain fields which were once havens of wildlife bear witness to the tragedy which has unfolded. To walk such fields today reveals a barren wasteland; barely a blackberry can be found; barely a wildflower; barely a butterfly. And the silent copses, hedges and empty skies all tell their own story. My children will never know the joy and awe engendered by the richness which the countryside once bestowed. Newton Harcourt's last rookery, located alongside the Grand Union Canal, was shot out by a local landowner at the height of the breeding season some fifty years ago and the birds did not return until the breeding season of 2011. During the mid 1970s, an entire wood was cut down (Barn Spinney) alongside the bridalway, which connects Newton Harcourt's village square with The Mere. Even as recently as fifteen years ago we could throw an old stale loaf onto the terrace at Elms Farm and the bread would be consumed within an hour. Now, the remnants can lie for days and the crumbs will, as often as not, be washed away by rain rather than eaten by small birds.

During the summer of 2003 I visited the Irish Republic and in Kildare met a seasoned countryman of some seventy years. He mentioned the appalling state of the Irish countryside, and described it as a barren wasteland and said that in twenty years time the only wildlife to be seen would be in the pages of a book. An exaggeration of course but his words contained a chilling ring of truth. I believe that nothing will bring back the splendour we knew, even thirty years ago.

Newton Harcourt however, is fortunate in having a wide range of habitats; woodland, canal and river; ponds; farmland and railway embankments, all of which have their own species of flora and fauna. Newton Harcourt received a further boost with the building of a lake at the western edge of the village. This has attracted grebes, ducks, geese and waders. The lake has also been stocked with a diversity of aquatic plants. In winter,

up to six different species of gulls can be seen in the area around the lake and before twilight on the short winter afternoons, the birds assemble into flocks and fly eastwards in V formation to the reservoirs of the Eyebrook and Rutland Water, where they spend the night. Woodcock are also to be seen in the damp low-lying woodland of Islands Spinney and Flaxman's Spinney.

It was G. K. Chesterton who said: "The mind should be a storehouse of sunsets". And to see flocks of several dozen Canada Geese coming in to land on Newton Harcourt's lake with a blazing sunset reflected in the water resembles one of Sir Peter Scott's exotic oil paintings.

In 2008, a national survey of otters revealed that they were five times more common than had been thought and it

Above: Winter Aconite in the Manor Spinney is clearly visible from the Newton to Wistow road.

Left: Delightful to behold, delightful to eat – Mirabelle plums harvested at Elms Farm.

Left page: The Mirabelle plum tree in the ancient hedge at Elms Farm. The exceptionally heavy crop of 2011 caused much joy and excitement at Elms.

has recently been announced that they have returned to every county in England. Certainly they have come back to Newton Harcourt and have been seen on the banks of the River Sence as it flows through the manor spinney.

An abundance of wild flowers can still be found, even in the depths of winter when the crocuses and snowdrops are in full bloom. These contrast with the bright yellow Winter Aconite, which can be seen in the Manor Spinney from the Wistow road between the church and the bridge over the River Sence. This species is not native and was introduced for medicinal purposes in the 19th century. Another marvellous discovery was made at Elms Farm when, in the ancient hedge separating the orchard from the paddock, two Mirabelle plum trees appeared. The fruits are round and bright yellow when ripe. They are particularly associated with the Lorraine region of France but they also occur in Romania and Hungary. They are sweet and beautifully flavoured and perfect for eating fresh or for the production of jam and pies. The juice of Mirabelles is also commonly used for wine making in addition to the fruits being used to make prunes.

Amid the butterflies to be seen in Newton Harcourt are Speckled Wood, which is unique amongst British species in hibernating sometimes as larvae and sometimes as pupa. Speckled woods were in decline for sixty years from the 1930s but have re-established themselves in recent years. They seek out bramble flowers and prefer the wooded and more shaded areas.

Another success story is the increase in raptors with buzzards and hobby now both breeding in the parish, along with a population of sparrow hawks, whose ferocity makes a kestrel appear like a jenny wren. There is clearly much to incite wonder.

This volume could be followed by a book on the Natural History of Newton Harcourt similar to that of "The Natural History of Selborne" by the Rev. Gilbert White. Published in 1788, this book has become a classic work. A similar volume on Newton Harcourt would be as illuminating in a hundred years time as it would be today.

Newton Harcourt has a resident population of kingfisher all the year round to the sheer joy of the many people lucky enough to see one.

Speckled Wood butterfly.

Otters can be spotted on the river banks around Newton Harcourt.

Tree Sparrows are immediately recognisable from their House Sparrow relations by their smaller size and chocolate coloured crowns. Thirty years ago, the two species were probably the most numerous in the area, often joining together to form vast flocks. Today, both are in serious decline.

All three British woodpeckers can be seen (or heard) on a walk through the village environs. The Greater and Lesser Spotted and the Green. The distinctive 'yaffle' cry of the Green Woodpecker contrasts with the drumming of the two spotted species.

Chaffinches are a much loved species throughout the area covered by this book.

Above: One of Newton Harcourt's increasing population of Sparrow hawks.

Left: The appearance of Great Crested Grebes on Newton Harcourt's lake has made a welcome addition to the village's list of species.

This scene, looking east, was made in 1965 from the Wigston to Fleckney road bridge. In the years leading up to 1965 there had been a marked reduction in the number of steam trains and the grass on the charred embankments was already beginning to regenerate. Elms Farm can be seen on the left, appropriately framed between two elm trees. All six of the stately elm trees visible in the scene were to die of Dutch Elm Disease along with three more on the left just outside the picture; in the late 1940s these three contained a small rookery. None have been replaced. In the immediate foreground is the colour signal for northbound trains whilst the 'Permanent Way' hut in the centre of the picture stands on the site of Newton Harcourt signal box which was closed during the 1930s. The gate on the right leads into the Lock House meadow. The bridge in the centre distance is the village bridge and the old school house and railway bridge on the Wistow road can be seen behind it.

This picture was taken almost fifty years later in the summer of 2011 from exactly the same camera position. It shows dramatically the reforestation of the embankments with their rich resources for flora and fauna. The railway embankments at Wigston have become a rich habitat for the rare Marbled White butterfly. Both the colour signal and the 'Permanent Way' hut have gone although the gate into the Lock House meadow remains the same as do the branches of the fir trees protruding into the picture from the top right.

The Great Crested Newt survives in Newton Harcourt albeit in an area with no public access.

Water forget – me – nots occur in clumps along the River Sence sometimes flowering until December. The related Wood forget – me – not is also found in Newton Harcourt.

Blackberry and apple is a traditional British delicacy, doubly so, the wild berries being so beneficial to health. This spray reveals the five development stages: bud open, open blossom and green, red and black fruit.

istow

By Joe Goddard

About one and a half miles south of Newton Harcourt lies Wistow Hall, the 'stately home' of the locality, which stands at the centre of the Wistow Estate.

The Hall itself lies at the heart of a small and pretty hamlet of converted traditional service buildings, all now residential and estate premises. The Hall which is on the site of a medieval manor house has been altered and added to over the years. It was bought by Sir Andrew Halford in 1603, who retained the original cellars and some foundations. It originally had 5 visible gables and it would have looked the perfect Elizabethan or early Jacobean manor house lying to the north west of the small and decreasing village of Wistow which was finally depopulated in the late 18th century. At about that time the Hall, which was built in random limestone was plastered (the plaster is called 'stucco' when applied to a house like this). Early in the 19th century the gables were replaced by hipped Swithland slate roofs set behind the distinct parapet we see today. There was a series of 3 medieval manor fishponds and Sir Henry Halford who inherited Wistow in 1813 drained one and enlarged another to form the present Wistow pond, at the same time diverting the Kibworth - Fleckney road to its present position. The Hall and pond together make a picture postcard English scene from the road.

Across the road, to the north, the picture is completed by the church of St Wiston at the end of its gravel drive. This is the mother church of the churches of Newton Harcourt, Kilby and Flekney. It is said to stand on the site of the murder of the heir to the throne of Mercia, Prince Wiston in 849 AD. The nave and chancel are much older than their classical 18th century appearance would suggest. The church dates from the 12th century (the site is almost certainly much older, of course). It was enlarged in 1300 and later in the 14th and 15th centuries and finally remodelled (but not rebuilt) in the 18th century. The tower is mainly 15th century.

About a quarter of a mile to the west of the settlement there is a small brick structure standing in the fields beside the Wigston - Fleckney road. This was built in the 1870s by the 3rd Sir Henry Halford, the last of the Halfords who became the first chairman of Leicestershire County Council. It is the firing point on a rifle range where new experimental rifles were tested over a range of 1000 yards, firing at a target beside the canal. The very first Lee Enfield rifles are reputed to have been tested there. The target, made of iron, still stands beside the canal. It pre-dates telephones, so some method had to be found of letting the shooter know that the bull's eye had been hit. There was a neat solution; the bulls eye rings like a gong when

Wistow church can look very remote in the depths of the Sence Valley, with the River Sence meandering by. The church is said to be on the site of the murder of Prince Wistan of Mercia in 849AD.

hit by anything – it's called a 'ringing target'; it's the last one in Britain. Access to it is easy as it lies beside the Newton Harcourt footpath to Kilby. If you throw a stone at it, you'll be surprised by the loud "bong".

The Wistow to Kilby road was closed to traffic on days when firing was in progress and a large red flag was flown from a pole in the field between the hut and the target although there was probably not much danger as bullets, at that point in their flight, would be about 40 feet up. (This curving flight of a bullet is called the trajectory). But there is no record of the canal or towpath being closed and it's possible to find bullets in the field across the canal opposite the target. These rounds would have whistled over canal, towpath and slow moving boat traffic at a height of about 3 or 4 feet, making a memorable trip for the canal user – if they had not seen the red flag!

The range was closed in the late 1930s. The little brick firing hut was revived in the early 1950s as an outlet for plants, vegetables and eggs from the home farm and kitchen garden at Wistow, as well as sweets, ice cream and pots of tea for the newly mobile visitors to 'Wistow Park' from Leicester. (The real Wistow Park lies between Wistow Hall and the Wigston to Fleckney road, The popularly termed Wistow Park is really called 'The Nooks'. However the word 'park' is incorrect as it implies an enclosed deer park which Wistow never had).

The little shop in the shooting hut grew and grew. First it moved into some farm buildings at Wistow and there it grew into the thriving rural centre that is at Wistow today, attracting thousands of visitors every year

Above: Wistow Hall, for 250 years the seat of the Halford family: then inherited by Lord Cottesloe and given to his granddaughter Lady Brooks in the early 1950s. The hall and its lake (known locally as Wistow Pond) make an idyllic English scene.

Left page: Even in the cold winters of the early twentieth century it was rarely possible to skate on Wistow Pond – an event captured in this rare picture.

The little building by the cross roads at Wistow where the first Lee Enfield rifles were fired at a target 1000 yards away.
Much later it became a shop selling pots of tea, ice cream and sweets to many weekend visitors from the suburbs.
This humble activity was the origin of a garden centre from which today's Rural Centre was born.

*The Rural Centre at Wistow brings a touch of
modernity into a timeless landscape. The large garden
centre is augmented by a wide range of craft shops along
with a model village and railway. The three acre site also
includes an excellent cafe serving a wide range of fare. In
season a maze is created from an adjoining crop field to
the delight of visitors from near and far.*

Music in the Park

by Colin Garratt

Music in the Park is an annual charity concert which takes place in the beuitiful grounds of Wistow Hall.

The 2012 event took place on 9th June and started with a dramatic flypast by an RAF Hawk advanced jet trainer. Participants bring their own picnics and enjoy the music which, in 2012, was provided by 'Junction 21' (an 18 piece swing band) and the award winning all female Brass Band 'Boobs and Brass'.

The event concludes at dusk with a fabulous firework display in front of Wistow Hall. Music in the Park is an event organised by Wigston Rotary Club on behalf of LOROS (Hospice care for Leicestershire and Rutland); Warning Zone (Leicestershire and Rutland Crimebeat Ltd) and the Breast Cancer Campaign. Each year the grounds of Wistow Hall are made available for the event by kind permission of the Brooks family. These occasions are not to be missed; the atmospher is all embracing and in 2012, £8000 was raised for the charities.

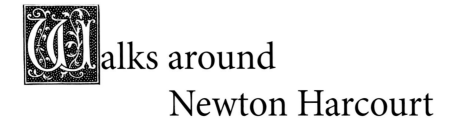alks around
Newton Harcourt

By Gina Handsley

The walks around Newton Harcourt are well renowned in the area. Described below are a few of them. Please refer to the map at the end of the chapter for the route bearings.

A. Wistow Road to Island Woods

Start by parking in the car park at the Rural Centre at Wistow. Take the country road (Wistow Road), bordered by laid, mixed hawthorn hedging, away from Wistow, towards Newton Harcourt. After about 400m take a moment to pause at the bridge over the river Sence looking across the ridge and furrow fields over to the Grand Union Canal. Mainly hidden by a mound and a wood at this point, designed to protect the sensibilities of the local gentry from the intrusion of this industrial waterway – how times change!

Continuing you pass on your left Island Woods, part of the grounds of Newton Harcourt manor. In late winter the wood floor is a picture of yellow aconites lighting up the shade.

B. Newton Harcourt Manor & St Lukes Church

The next point of interest is St Lukes Church, (see p74) constructed in several building styles from the 10th through to the 19th centuries. The churchyard has a number of interesting headstones and also provides another glorious floral display in early Spring with its mass covering of snowdrops. The Manor house opposite - which again spans many centuries - probably originated during the 12th and 13th centuries and has some interesting tales to tell.

Walkers taking the field route from Newton Harcourt to Wistow.

C. Canal & Railway Bridges

Continue on to arrive at the 2 great arteries from the Industrial Revolution which run parallel at this point. Walk onto Newton bridge (Number 80), and to your left you will see the old Lock Keeper's cottage and locks which offers an alternative leg along the canal to this walk. Cross over the railway bridge (SPC 3/9) where it is likely you will witness the speeding by of the mainline London train to or from St Pancras – an interesting contrast to the gentle walk you are currently on. A wave from the bridge often elicits a rewarding toot!

D. Old School House, Old Post Office & Village Well

Turn left onto a footpath that runs alongside the railway line, walk along this until you reach Post Office Lane. Turn right at the Old School House. and past the old Post Office opposite the red telephone kiosk – no longer in use in this mobile age, and original village well, 110 ft deep, fed by a natural spring and currently being restored. (Within a hundred yards on the bend of Post Office Lane you will see a footpath on your right which takes you across ancient meadows to Wistow Road, point H of the walk)

E. The Square

From Post Office lane turn left onto the footpath running alongside the garden wall of Old Croft Farm. As you exit the jitty you will notice on your right the pump in the square which was fed by the Well and still in use as recently as the 1950's. The long house completing 'the square', facing you as you look left on exiting the jitty, is Sycamore House, which in a previous life was the local hostelry and known originally as The Bull and subsequently as The Recruiting Sergeant during the Napoleonic Wars.

The view to the west from bridge No. 79 showing the old lock keeper cottage.

Below: The village water pump located in the Square, prior to renovation by the Friends of Newton Harcourt.

Right: The old village telephone situated in Post Office Lane permanently lit from the adjacent house. Old Croft Farm is silhouetted in the background.

F. Milepost 92 1/2

Walk past the water pump out of the square and turn left into Glen Road, take care walking alongside the road for about 100 yards. On the right hand side you will see the replica Midland Railway Milepost 92 1/2 indicating the distance from Newton Harcourt to London St Pancras. Opposite the Milepost is Elms Farm House. On the high chimney can be seen a weathervane based on one of Colin Garratt's pictures of a Swiss built locomotive he photographed in Argentina. Turn right at the footpath beyond the Milepost and make your way diagonally across the fields towards Newton Lane and the pumping station. You will be able to see the large irrigation lake in the near distance -used to ensure a good crop of potatoes (A short detour to take a look at the lake offers a wonderful sight of seasonally changing wildlife).

G. Octagon Cottages

Retrace your steps to Glen Road and turn left, within 120 yards Octagon Cottages, appears on your left which in the past was 2 toll houses (now made into 1)where drovers paid a toll to water their cattle at the watering hole at the rear of the property.

H. Wistow Road and back to the bridges

Cross over the main road and continue along, past Hursts Farm on your right. Turn right back into Wistow Road. Within a hundred yards you will see a footpath on your right which takes you along the historical route across ancient meadows back to Post Office Lane and the centre of the village. For this route however, continue along the road back over the railway bridge and at the canal bridge take the steps down to the waterway. Turn left along the towpath (with St Lukes church on your right). Keep your eyes peeled for the flora and fauna, a flash of irredescent blue is likely to be a kingfisher beating a hasty retreat.

I. High Bridge & St Wistan's Church

Continue and pass under bridge number 79 called High Bridge, you will see St Wistan's Church in the distance, named after the Mercian Royal Prince martyred here in 849 ad. Continue along the tow path until you reach bridge 78, take the steps away from the towpath on your left immediately before the bridge, turn right over the bridge. Follow the footpath across the meadows and the River Sence towards the church. On crossing the river take the footpath left into the churchyard and out onto Kibworth Road noting the beauty of the setting. Turn right at the road.

(Below in the 'Variation' section you will find an alternative suggestion for a walk to the village of Fleckney)

J. Wistow Pond

The walk at this point goes right, but initially take a slight detour left as you cross the road and enjoy the wildfowl and swans cruising on Wistow Manor Pond with Wistow Hall standing grandly in the background. Turn back and continue along the road until you return to the Wistow Rural Centre for well deserved refreshment and shopping.
Relax!

The stile leading from the ancient meadow. Post Office Lane lies behind the distant hedge and Old Croft Farm in the background.

The railway footpath which leads from the Wistow Road back to the village bridge.

Variations based on the above walks.

Variation E: On exiting the jitty into The Square turn left and walk along the road over the railway bridge until you reach the footpath sign. Cross the field down to the canal locks reached through the gate beside the Lock House. Turn right onto the canal bank and follow the tow path :

    1. To the Navigation public house at Kilby Bridge - follow the tow path under Wain Bridge, passing Top Half-Mile Lock, over Turnover Bridge, Tythorn Bridge and Clifton Bridge until you reach Kilby Bridge and the popular public house for a spot of food and drink.

    2. To the Dog and Gun public house in Kilby - follow the tow path passing under Wain Bridge. At which point you

need to get across to the opposite side of the canal. Immediately take the path on your right off the tow path onto Newton Lane, turn right to cross the bridge then turn right back to rejoin the footpath crossing the stile, again heading towards Kilby. Continue past Newton Bottom Lock. Ahead is a delightful walk through Flaxman's Spinney. Follow the signs through the riding stables. You should catch sight on your right of the last surviving example of a ringing rifle target, believed to be unique to Britain. Then cross the gallops (keeping your eyes peeled!) and onwards across the fields and finally crossing the bridge over the River Sence towards the stile over to your left on Fleckney Road. Turn right and follow the road via Main Street into the village where you fill find the watering hole and eatery of the Dog and Gun on your left.

Above: Turnover Bridge on the way from Newton Harcourt to Kilby Bridge.

Left page: Britain's last 'ringing target'. The black bullseye gives a loud 'Bong' when struck by a stone (or bullet). The shooting-box is still there, about 1000 yards away (p106). A scene on the walk from Newton Harcourt to Kilby.

Variation F1. To Oadby - Instead of turning left out of The Square, cross Glen Road and continue straight on along the Bridle path (the old Saxon way) towards Oadby. It was in this area during World War 2 that decoy fires were prepared ready to distract the focus of German bombers. Keeping the hedgerow on your left, follow the path up the rise, passing at the highest point a spinney on your right. Continue until you reach the waymark post at which point turn left and once again follow the hedgerow on your left until you reach Mere Lane. Turning right at this point takes you onto Mere Lane, past the riding stables and towards the edge of Oadby.

Above: A Constablesque view of the path leading to Newton Harcourt as seen from The Mere.
Walkers from both Glen Gorse and Wigston will pass this way.

Top left: The arcadian joys of the Mere.

Left: The parting of the ways along the Mere.

Variation F2.- To Wigston Magna - instead of turning left out of The Square, cross Glen Road and continue straight on along the Bridle path (the old Saxon way) towards Oadby. Keeping the hedgerow on your left, follow the path up the rise, passing at the highest point a spinney on your right. Continue until you reach the waymark post at which point turn left and once again follow the hedgerow on your left until you reach Mere Lane. Turning right at this point onto Mere Lane and almost immediately you will see on your left the Waymark post which takes you across the golf course. Pay attention to wayward golf balls! Continue to fol low the signs across arable fields taking an almost straight path until you reach the outer edge of Wigston Magna.

Variation I. To Fleckney - instead of turning off the canal to St Wistan's church continue along the towpath which shortly becomes an aqueduct over a small stream making an interesting diversion to your walk. At Crane's Lock cross the canal and continue on the footpath to reach the road. Cross the road and follow the footpath signs again across fields passing Wistow Grange Farm on your left into Fleckney village for a range of shops and pubs.

Above: This magnificent oak dominates the landscape on the final approaches to Wigston.

Left page: Lesser Whitethroat territory on the path from Wigston Magna to The Mere.

The sedate progress of a narrowboat heading south from Newton Harcourt contrasts to the passing Inter City 125 which upon their inception were the fastest diesel trains in the world.

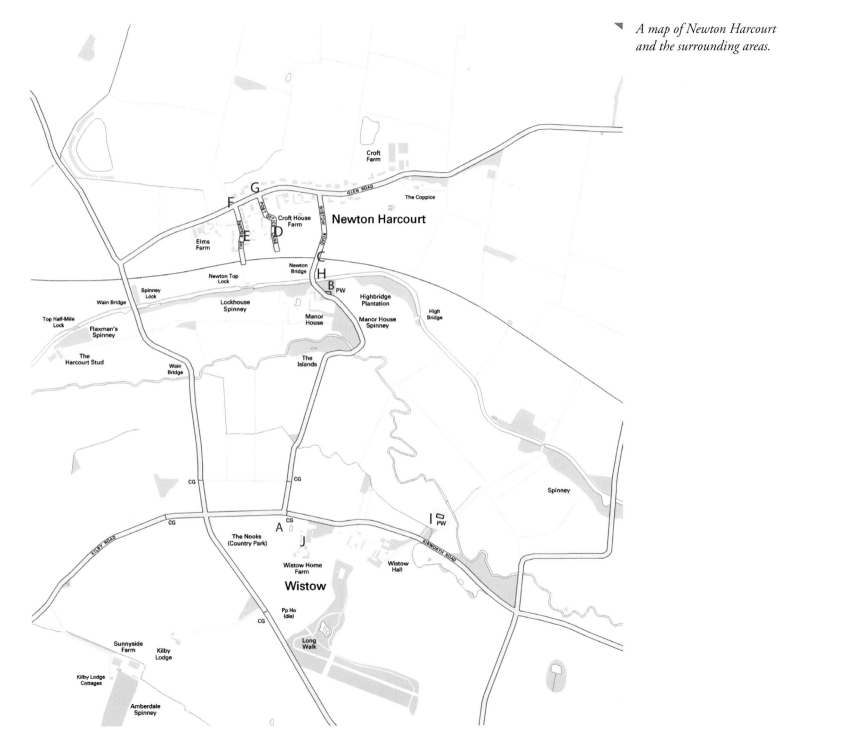

A map of Newton Harcourt and the surrounding areas.

The Friends of Newton Harcourt

By Colin Garratt

The Friends of Newton Harcourt (FNH) was founded in 1978 by Colin Garratt. The inaugural meeting in the village hall was well attended and over 50 people 'signed up' to become members. The organisation was, from the outset, conservation based and the opening charter was hard hitting and focussed on preventing the spoliation of the village and the surrounding countryside. A few months after the FNH's formation Colin Garratt left on a six month expedition to Latin America and Maurice Williams succeeded him as chairman. The 1970s were a time of rapid change in England; villages were under the increasing threat of urbanisation whilst intensive farming was a growing threat to the traditional beauty and diversity of the countryside.

The FNH has been a vigorous organisation since its inception and is now a registered charity. One of the early achievements was to take over the management of Gypsy Wood located alongside the road from Great Glen into Newton Harcourt.

Groups of FNH members cover the village trimming hedges and verges and planting trees. Flowers have been distributed around the village including many wild species. Any rubbish which has accrued or been dumped is taken away. Memorial seats have been set in place along with a beautifully crafted village notice board and in the autumn of 2011 the timberwork encasing the water pump in the village square was renewed.

The FNH has always shown a great flair for fundraising and this has enabled them to grant money to the Village Hall Fund and the Church in addition to their conservation activities. All residents of Newton Harcourt now have automatic membership of the FNH.

In the near future, the FNH intends to fulfil a long-term ambition to restore the water pump in the square to working order. Apart from being a delightful amenity this would make a historical link to the days when over a dozen pumps were active around the village. These were not displaced until 1953 when mains water reached the village.

Left: Gwen Ingham's memorial seat complete with plaque placed by the FNH alongside the railway footpath.

The refurbished pump in the village square.

FNH logo

Newton Harcourt in the future

By Colin Garratt

Newton Harcourt is an amenity village which attracts visitors from the suburbs of Oadby and Wigston and further afield from Leicester itself. The village possesses a rare combination of attractions embracing:

Social History: Newton Harcourt Manor, St Luke's Church, St Wistan's Church Wistow, Wistow Hall and lake

Industrial History: the canal and the railway

Agricultrial History: dating back for 1000 years

Natural History: crowned by otters, kingfishers and buzzards along with a plethora of other wildlife seen in a magnificent rural setting.

It is a triumph of our planning system that Newton Harcourt has retained its charm. My association with the village began in 1949 and little has changed structurally since then: the village's architectural beauty remains undiminished and its long sweeping views into the surrounding countryside also remain intact and unspoiled. Few places – in a world of ever increasing development and urbanisation – could make such a claim.

But threats are ever present. In 1996 an important three acre field within the village lost its 'Important Open Land' status (which would make development impossible). The meadow has now been designated 'agricultural land': an altered status which would make it potentially easier to develop. Such a move would create an implant of urbanisation which would scar the village's identity. The site is kept under review thanks to an efficient village planning committee.

It is essential that rural communities adjacent to large conurbations be treated with great sensitivity. Newton Harcourt is so close to Leicester and its suburbs that at night the glow of the city's lights to the north are a dominant feature, the village having no street lighting. And yet, when in Newton Harcourt, one could almost be in the country of Hardy's Wessex novels. This is environmental magic.

Many of Newton Harcourt's residents, including the thirty year old Friends of Newton Harcourt, have a strong sense of custodianship and feel a responsibility to help maintain the village's enchantment for future generations. This book is published in the hope that it will encourage a wider interest in and awareness of the village, as well as appealing to its many well-wishers far beyond the parish boundary. This will help to ensure that Newton Harcourt is seen and maintained as the microcosm of Old England that it is. And with Old England's greatness enshrined therein.

Development! Why the village must be watchful.

Newton Harcourt Pig Club

By Colin Garratt

During World War Two it was Germany's dream that food shortages in Britain would debilitate the nation and lead to a German victory. The risk of this Nazi ideal becoming reality gave rise to the 'Dig for Victory' campaign and railway embankments and wasteland all over Britain were turned into allotments. A boost in the production of livestock was also undertaken and in 1941 as part of this national movement Newton Harcourt established a Pig Club. The following is a verbatim account from the Newton Harcourt Pig Club record and accounts book of that year:

'A meeting was held in the Reading Room on April 1st and was very well attended by all interested and was very pleasant and very cheerful. The members choosing Miss Smart as Chairwomen and Louisa Scotchbrook as secretary. Mr Freckleton kindly let us have one of his buildings which

we are all very grateful for. 10 members joined and we decided to have 5 pigs from Mr Smart. The members being willing to bring pigswill to the barn, potatoe peelings, fresh grass, cabbage leaves and lettuce to give to the pigs. It was also decided to give Mr Ellingworth a shilling a week to feed them and clean them out so now we have 5 nice pigs and Mr Smart has kindly given us straw for the manure to be put back on his manure heap which I am sure all members are very grateful to him. We also decided to insure our piggys for 3 shillings a head amounting to 15 shillings so if one did happen to pass over all would not be lost. So this has been done and we have got the policy back'.

We also were successful and got 2 'truffs' for the pigs' feed and members all decided to pay 2 shillings a week for the present time and time being.

Southbound Diesel

New image, capital bound
Through suburban intrigue intrepidly threads
Rhythmically whirring through soot lined tunnels
Tension mounts as the track gleams ahead

Snaking southwards with a fearsome whine
Scarring pastoral scenes with an arrow of blue
Acrid fumes tint the soft wayside air
Disdainful of nature's balanced hue

Counties unfold in tumultuous passage
Past villages serene technology roars
A cry from the klaxon seeps through the woodlands
Animals canter and wild birds soar

With coaches screaming on ribboned steel
All resistance the climaxing Sultzer defies
A three figured whirlwind howls down the valley
Old railway builders' dreams personified.

Colin Garratt, 1970

The visual manifestation of the 1970 poem "Southbound Diesel" as a three figured whirlwind howls through the village cutting.

Rural Apparitions

By Colin Garratt

At the beginning of the year, scarecrows preside over early sowings of rape and wheat. It is a time when the weather is most inclement; battering winter gales, driving rain and sleet, or damp, cold mists. Many scarecrows get blown into weird positions like drunken men; others collapse and vanish from view. Some stand firm only to be partially dismembered by the wind with pieces of their anatomy spread far and wide. It is not uncommon for passers-by to attack a scarecrow; stabbing and mutilations being the most common.

Scarecrows with guns make convincing marksmen. With generations of birds having been shot since time immemorial, it may be assumed that a figure with a gun is the ideal deterrent. If his body swivels round in the wind enabling the gun to be pointed in all directions so much the better. Most gun-bearing scarecrows are made with great conviction and represent a preferable alternative to the degrading practice of shooting birds.

The variety of scarecrows is infinite and all have their character. Some stand with arms and legs stiff. Others are a ripple of movement, some root into the ground like a tree; others stride across the fields waving flags. Yet more hang from gibbets, twisted into hideous shapes. Others are hoisted on poles. From Medieval times, the classic location was on the brow of a hill eerily silhouetted against the sky; a warning presence by day and a frightening spectre at dusk. Without the scarecrow's haunting presence, our landscape would be greatly impoverished.

Newton Harcourt's medieval roots were dramatically recalled by these genuine working scarecrows. The spectre's appearance on the eastern end of the village during the early 1990s was a direct desendent of similar apparitions which have haunted the landscape for centuries. A remarkable occurrence in the age of high-tech farming, albeit that the hubcap head induces an eerie note of modernity. Genuine scarecrows are on the verge of extinction although stragglers can still be found in muddy isolation, largely unseen amid the elements.

The Meadows of Newton Harcourt

**A reflection from long-time resident of Newton Harcourt,
Mike Lockwood**

I moved to Newton Harcourt in 1970. The village was quiet and off
the beaten track; very little traffic!

The land around Newton Harcourt had three farms
belonging to Edgar Smart, Wallace Kenny and Fred Oakey. These
farms had been worked by the same farming methods used before
World War Two. Pastures were left to grow naturally as the farms
were all dairy farms.

Edgar Smart had a number of fields which had not been
disturbed since the turn of the nineteenth century. These water
meadows were on the west of the village bordering the Wigston
Lane. At about 15 to 20 acres, these two meadows had been left to
grow naturally for over 100 years. Wild flowers were abundant and
there was a natural stream running through the fields over which
were willows and a bridge. The stream had watercress growing in it,
which was very good with salad for the numerous picnics we had in
the meadows.

The fields were like a long-forgotten memory, where grew
Ragged Robin, bee orchids, red clover, sorrel, poppy, cranesbills,
meadow buttercup, wild geranium, cowslips, cornflowers, daisies
and many types of meadow grass. It was an idyllic place for children's
picnics and a place to sit and relax and let the world pass by. All has
now, sadly, disappeared under modern agriculture.

Above: Meadow Buttercups.

Left page: Bee orchid

Diamond Jubilee Celebration

Held in the Lock House meadow 3rd June 2012

By Colin Garratt

Queen Elizabeth II's Diamond Jubilee celebrations will be remembered as being one of the most momentous events in British history. Newton Harcourt staged its own celebration in the very finest of the village's traditions. It was an event which brought the community together and for those old enough to remember, evoked memories of village characters who are no longer with us. The marquee was situated alongside the path which the 'Dairylea Girl' (p68) used to walk on her way from the Lock House to the water pump in The Square.

But watching the village's children play their games and dance to the pulsating rhythms of the band one thought of the generations to come, as inevitably they must. It is hoped that they will continue to be enchanted by both our monarchy and village.

Heavy rain fell throughout much of Britain on Queen Elizabeth's Diamond Jubilee Day and not least in Newton Harcourt. This is the view across the Lock House Meadow from the village railway bridge. Instead of picnicking outside over a hundred villagers were confined to the marquee. But there was no dampening of spirit and even when the last revellers faded away into the darkness shortly before midnight the deluge showed no sign of abating.

The following morning after the marquee was dismantled, the sun shone again evoking poignant memories of an unforgettable day.

The Authors wish to acknowledge the support of:

Nigel Allcoat - Sponser
Michael Kellett - Sponser
Roger and Linda Grzyb
David and Cheryl Bishop
Heather Macdermid
David and Annie James
Glenys, Craig and Annette Handford
Sue Bloy and Steven Swindon
Samantha and Tim Osorio
Matt and Jenny Wilson
Graham and Gloria Wilson
Brian and Lindsey Jarman
Mark Cass
Nigel and Lynn Dickinson
Tony and Jacqueline Toland
John Goodacre Esq. and Stephanie Goodacre
Julian Goodacre
Pamela, Rachael, Andrew and Rebecca Herbert
Jill Rickard, Trevor Vendy, Emma Walker, John Walker
Bob and Pat Clayton
Roger and Margaret Jones, Tim Hubbard
Helen Newell
Lisa Green
Wendy Brown
Diana Lee
Keith and Nora Cooper
Mr JW Baker

James Alvey
Dr and Mrs Jameson, Robert Jameson and Elizabeth Jameson
Walter, Norman and David Tyrell
George and Pamela Weston
Richard Brooks
Mike, Rachel, Amanda, David and Mark Lockwood
Graham and Gina Handsley
Diane Taylor
David and Catriona Scott
Michael Parker
Anthony Goddard Esq.
Graham and Jo Mansfield
The Reverend Canon Philip O'Reilly, SSC
William Scotchbrook
Alf and Sheila Roberts
Andy, Pauline and Maxine Winston
Josie Wragg
Dennis and Ann Partridge
Alena Burton
Christopher Hilton
Barry and Liz Ellwood
David and Donna Baker
Leslie Parr
Jack Hire
Graham and Halina McDowell
Cred & Sue Hughes

MILEPOST

Credits & Acknowledgements

All pictures in this book are credited to Milepost with the exception of the following:

Mick Freakley: p96 left and p97 all images
Old Union Canal Society: p1, p54
Leicestershire County Records Office: p55, p59
Sheila Grzyb: p41 left
Marie-Louise Garratt: p101 top & bottom
The late Judy Ashcroft: p83
Tim Graham: p90
Mitch Grzyb: p41 right
Roger Grzyb: p42 & p43

The publishers wish to record their thanks for the use of the above pictures and also to Sir Tim and Lady Brooks for their assistance with the Wistow chapter. We would also like to thank Sacrewell Farm and Country Centre, Peterborough.

Published in 2012 by Milepost Publishing, Newton Harcourt, Leicestershire, LE8 9FH
Design: Milepost 92 ½
Printed by Gutenberg Press Ltd
ISBN: 978 -1 -900193 -75 -7